B

Please Don't Die! But If You Do, What Do I Do Next?

A *Practical* and Cost-Saving Guide for the Estate Executor

by

Keith S. Grube, Esq.,

and

Kurt J. Grube

with John E. Nevola

ISBN: 1-4752-8219-2
ISBN-13: 978-1-4752-8219-1
LCCN: 2012907975
174 Packard Avenue Wyckoff, New Jersey 07481 USA

To Kathy, Kelly and Chris

The authors have taken great care in the preparation and writing of this book. It is based solely on the authors' opinions regarding estate administration. The authors are in no way offering legal, accounting, tax, and/or any other professional advice. Although best efforts have been made in preparing this book, the authors make no representations or warranties of any kind and assume no liabilities of any kind with respect to the accuracy or completeness of the contents and specifically disclaim any implied warranties or fitness of use for a particular purpose. The authors shall not be held liable or responsible to any person or entity with respect to any loss or incidental or consequential damages caused, or alleged to have been caused, directly or indirectly, by the information or programs contained herein. Every situation is different, and the advice and strategies contained herein may not be suitable for your particular situation. You should seek the services of a competent professional before undertaking the administration of an estate. References to actual persons, either living or dead, is strictly coincidental.

Foreword

This is the second edition of "Please Don't Die" updating for changes since the original was penned in 2012 and incorporates inputs from readers feedback over the prior 10 or so years. Both editions of this book are an outgrowth of the frustration we experienced as executors with the lack of practical, detailed information for people upon whom the responsibility of being the executor or executrix[1] for an estate has been placed. It represents a compilation of lessons learned and facts unearthed from our own personal perspectives, the result being a process an executor can follow as he or she administers the estate. We also wanted to offer some practical perspectives on, quite frankly, how to save money in the process.

Navigating through this experience, it seemed as if there should have been a plethora of help for an executor closing a large estate. There weren't many books on the subject, and the Internet was extraordinarily confusing. A lawyer may be more than helpful in closing an estate; however, unless it's very large, lawyers tend to get very costly very quickly. Lawyers are helpful in that they understand the complexities of closing a large and/or complex estate, because that's what they do. They also spend considerable amounts of time doing so, which translates into high cost. An estate lawyer may also be very helpful in small, noncomplex estates; however, there is still a cost associated with engaging a lawyer. The point here is that you can do most of the work of closing out an estate by yourself with just a little help from a lawyer which may result

---

[1] Executor is male and executrix is female. For simplicity the term 'executor' is used throughout the book

in a substantial cost savings for the estate. Putting the cost issue aside, and looking at it from a personal perspective, there is something distant and detached about engaging a lawyer in closing your loved ones estate; you are now relying on a stranger to understand the intimacy and grief that pervades every decision and tempers every judgment. There is something to be said for keeping the administration "in the family." This book was written for just that reason, so that you can keep the family involved and informed throughout the process.

We also wanted to write this book so that other people would not have to struggle in closing out their estate. One of the interesting aspects about closing an estate is that when it is finished, there is a sense of closure. It gives the feeling that you and the family can finally start to move on. You've also fulfilled the wishes of your loved one, and you can rest a bit easier knowing that you've carried those wishes out to the best of your ability. As it's been said, time heals all wounds, and closing out the estate tends to accelerate the healing process.

One might think that closing an estate is simply a matter of dividing up the money and moving on. It's not about that at all. Closing an estate is far from just splitting the money among the beneficiaries. That's the easy part. The tough part is the contention among the beneficiaries and non-beneficiaries for those "things" that had sentimental value. It's more about minimizing the anxiety and maintaining family bonds. It's about preventing any rupture to the relationships among the living. And one has to be prepared to relive the memories of the past as items of sentimental value are distributed.

We also wanted to help in reducing the amount of money it takes to close out an estate. The cost is typically in attorney fees and expenses. Most of the work the attorney does is administrative in nature, such as mailing letters, filling out forms, and making routine phone calls. They also execute a stock power, close out bank accounts, and write an IRA beneficiaries letter among many other items and then charging for those services. All these items add up, and many of them can be handled directly and easily by the executor.

To be clear, **<u>in no way are we suggesting not engaging an attorney</u>**. In fact, we feel that it is essential to use an attorney to handle even a small estate. What we are suggesting is that an attorney's time is better spent ensuring that the court and creditors have no problem with the estate during and after the closing. The attorney's time is not well spent performing administrative tasks that do not require their specialized skill. You need the lawyer to keep you between the process lines and the benefit of their insurance coverage if a mistake is made. An attorney would also know the specific procedures and laws applicable to different states as each have their own nuances.

This guide may seem a bit cold at times, but grief and the business of estate administration are two very different things. During the grieving process people are most vulnerable to making decisions they may regret (at best) and being taken advantage of (at worst). It is our sincere hope that this guide will give you the confidence to handle the responsibilities of an executor and avoid the pitfalls, and that it will save you time and money. Please feel free to contact us via our website 'www.executorbook.com' as we would be glad to try to answer any questions you may have.

This second edition published in 2021 includes many updates to various websites, processes and has incorporated feedback from comments left by many readers on Amazon. The authors welcome any feedback and will continue to update this guide over time.

One final note: the example spreadsheets and letters are all available on our website 'https://www.executorbook.com'. Click on 'Templates' and use the password "thebook" for access. If you have any feedback either positive or suggestions for improvement or would like to share your executor story for inclusion in the next edition - please feel free to send an e-mail to kjgrube@executorbook.com.

Glossary of Terms

Administrator	One who is responsible for making decisions for the estate
Attorney	A person whom you appoint to act for you
Codicil	A legal document that further explains something and/or makes changes to a will.
Decedent	The person who passed away
Descendant	A person who was a familial relation—for example, a child, grandchild, great-grandchild
Domicile	Where a person lived, where a person's home was—this is a person's legal residence
Estate	All the property that was owned by the decedent
Equal - Equitable	Equal is a "50/50" distribution, equitable is a "fair" distribution which may not be "50/50"
Executor	The person (male) named in the will selected to carry out the terms of the will
Executrix	The person (female) named in the will selected to carry out the terms of the will
Fiduciary	A person who is put in a position of trust and confidence
Intestate	Not making a will before one dies, if someone dies without a will they are said to have died "intestate"
Lawyer	Same as attorney

Letters Testamentary	A document that says the executor can act to close the will
Per Stirpes	Latin meaning each gets an equal share of the estate
Probate	When the surrogate court officially says the will is valid
Real Property	Tangible items such as a house, furniture, cars
Surrogate	The governmental official who has the authority to probate a will
Surrogate Court	The court that makes decisions about the validity of a will and resolves disputes among or between the Executor and beneficiaries (see probate)
Testate	Having a will when one dies
Testator	The person (male) who made the will
Testatrix	The person (female) who made the will
Transfer Agent	A company that tracks individuals and entities who own stock

TABLE OF CONTENTS

Chapter 1

First Things First

The following paragraphs are from the original edition and they still hold water. But in creating the second edition and really thinking about it, the very first thing a family should do is have a family meeting about what things should come first. The money from the estate will be disbursed as will the furniture, the house will be sold, the jewelry distributed - that's easy compared to the varying expectations from each of the beneficiaries. What to do? Put a big bottle of vodka on the table with the requisite number of glasses! That said - going around the table and having a discussion about the imminent, what to do for the funeral and how to put together the framework for the longer term, the overarching "we're all going to have to work together" and that leads into division of labor which includes everyone in the process. The last thing an executor wants is to have one of the siblings/beneficiaries feel left out of the process due to some perceived slight and then have hard feeling which result in people not speaking for months or years.

Administering an estate as an executor is a process. As with any process, there is a defined start and a defined end. One could argue that the process for an executor begins when a person writes their will and names their executor or executrix. It's not when the person who has written the will dies. As the one named as the executor, you may have the unique opportunity to discuss their wishes and wants with them before they pass away. Although this discussion may be difficult and feel a bit morbid, it is an excellent opportunity to discover and document how the person wants their final funeral wishes carried out, whether they want a large service or a small memorial, flowers or donations in lieu of them, burial versus cremation, and the many, many other arrangements and decisions that need to be made, and made very quickly, after the person passes.[2] As the executor, you are probably made responsible via the will for making the funeral arrangements for the deceased. If this is the case, you ought to know what they desire. If Aunt Bessie wanted to be cremated and you decide to bury her, you're running the risk of alienating everyone Aunt Bessie ever knew. At the end of the day, Aunt Bessie probably isn't going to be too concerned about whether she's on the fireplace mantel or six feet under once she heads on home to the Promised Land. You can bet, however, that if you don't follow what Aunt Bessie really wanted, her beneficiaries may make your life miserable. The point is, it's not about the money—money issues can be resolved; it's the feeling that you slighted Aunt Bessie that'll be remembered.

In fact, people writing their wills should create a checklist with their instructions for the funeral just to make sure that what they want to happen actually does happen. As noted above, nothing is worse than wanting to be buried in a small plot under the big tree but ending up cremated and spread out over the ocean. To prevent those types of issues from arising, people should consider the funeral home, the type of service, the burial clothing, which church, what type of church

[2]See Appendix A: Checklist for Funeral Arrangements.

service, the singers and accompaniment, flowers, donations, funeral home cards, limousines, a hearse, songs at the wake, the hours of the wake, and so on. It's easier to make those choices when you're alive than it is to have someone figure out what you wanted after you've passed on. An added plus is that you'll be remembered the way you want to be remembered. If you want the "under the big tree" burial, make sure someone knows about it now and write it down!

The person writing the will also has the opportunity to document the location of bank accounts, securities, funds, bonds, safety deposit boxes, life insurance policies, and so on. At a minimum, you, as the executor, should request that they secure all that information in a couple of places so that it is readily available when the time comes. Make sure that online access for accounts is also considered. Have your loved one write down URL's and passwords so that when the time comes, access is simple. You should also stress that you are not interested in seeing their personal information and do not want access to it. You don't have a need to know. What you as the executor do have the need for when your loved one passes is the ability to quickly and efficiently identify accounts, pay off bills, know who the beneficiaries are, manage and maintain any real-estate holdings, and so on. You have to have the information needed to manage another household.

Don't take the job lightly either. Being an executor can be a little bit overwhelming at first and requires a significant investment of time, emotion, and, to a lesser degree, money. The time and effort one must spend in the administration of an estate is considerable, especially in the beginning. Filling out forms, following up on issues, dealing with banks and brokerages, finding a real-estate agent to sell the house, attorney meetings, contacting creditors, working with hospitals, and so on all will take up a lot of your time. You could look at the alternative and engage an attorney. He or she could handle the administration, but they would obviously do it for a fee. With some estate lawyers' fee schedules at $30 for every six minutes, it can become very expensive for an attorney to handle such mundane matters. For example, let's say that the person who passed had ten different stocks. The lawyer might reasonably bill the estate $300 (or more) for the hour that it would take to simply print the forms, complete them, mail them, and follow up with you on the transfers. Each of those tasks takes a lawyer time, and they'll bill for it. Performing those simple tasks by yourself would save you a significant amount of money. On top of that, they'll take the executor fee. This can range from 5 to 20 percent in some states of the total gross estate, so going that route can get pretty costly pretty quickly.

The emotional part of being an executor also takes its toll. You are looked at as being solely responsible for the fair distribution of possessions and money. The distribution of money is usually easy because, quite frankly, it can be measured objectively. For example, if the estate is worth $100,000 in cash and there are two beneficiaries who share equally, each receives $50,000. Not too much to argue about in that scenario. What is far more difficult is the distribution of possessions. That is because of the arbitrary nature of the value of a possession. It's a very subjective matter to determine the value of Dad's favorite books and Mom's favorite clock. In spite of best intentions, there will likely be arguments over "who got more" because of the subjectivity of distribution.

In addition, beneficiaries are likely to try to determine what is fair. The difficult part is how to define fairness. Each person has his or her own definition of fairness, so what's fair to John may not be viewed as fair by Mary. Emotionally you must separate yourself from those types of arguments and conduct yourself reasonably, even though you are probably a beneficiary of the estate yourself. While this is happening, you are receiving advice (contradictory, of course) from friends, neighbors, and probably your spouse or partner. It's very difficult to put your emotions aside and conduct the administration as "only business, not personal."

Your own wealth also becomes a factor when you are named the executor. You're using your money to buy "stuff" as both a matter of convenience and to save the estate money. You'll be using your cash to purchase incidentals, possibly lending the estate money for funeral expenses, and paying for other unforeseen items as time goes on. You will do this rather than have the attorney distribute cash because of the fee structure noted above ($30 every six minutes). Of course you will be reimbursed by the estate for those items; however, you will be the one laying out the cash up front.

You need to be aware of those things before you agree to be the executor of an estate. Most people cannot foresee the amount of time they will spend administering the estate or anticipate the emotional roller coaster and the fact that they will be using their personal finances for the sake of expediency.

You are also in a position of great trust and great responsibility. You are a fiduciary and have a legal obligation to act as such. You will have access to bank accounts, securities, cash, and property that aren't yours—you are holding and administering them in trust for others. You will hear and read that you have a fiduciary responsibility to each of the beneficiaries. A fiduciary is a person who holds something in trust for another. You will be holding the estate and the distribution thereof in trust for the beneficiaries. It is essential that you behave with the utmost integrity, even in small matters. Your conduct must be beyond reproach.

You must also keep one overarching item in mind: *make sure you pay the government!* This means that you'll have to inform the Social Security Administration (SSA) that the person has died and that they should stop sending checks. Do that right away. You'll have to make sure that tax returns are filed properly. Make sure you focus on any item where the government is owed money. The government will be relentless in pursuing the estate and pursuing you as the executor if you try to avoid paying taxes, hide monies, and understate the value of items. It's just not worth the hassle or the threat of going to jail.

The following is a graphic of how an estate can be administered, starting *before* the person passes away. It's a relative timeline of the activities (at a high level) that should be accomplished. Notice that the majority of the activity takes place immediately after the person dies. There will be times in the beginning when the administration consumes countless hours of your time. After this initial thrust, however, the activity slows to a crawl as you wait for real estate to be sold, tax returns to be prepared, and other items with longer lag times to take place.

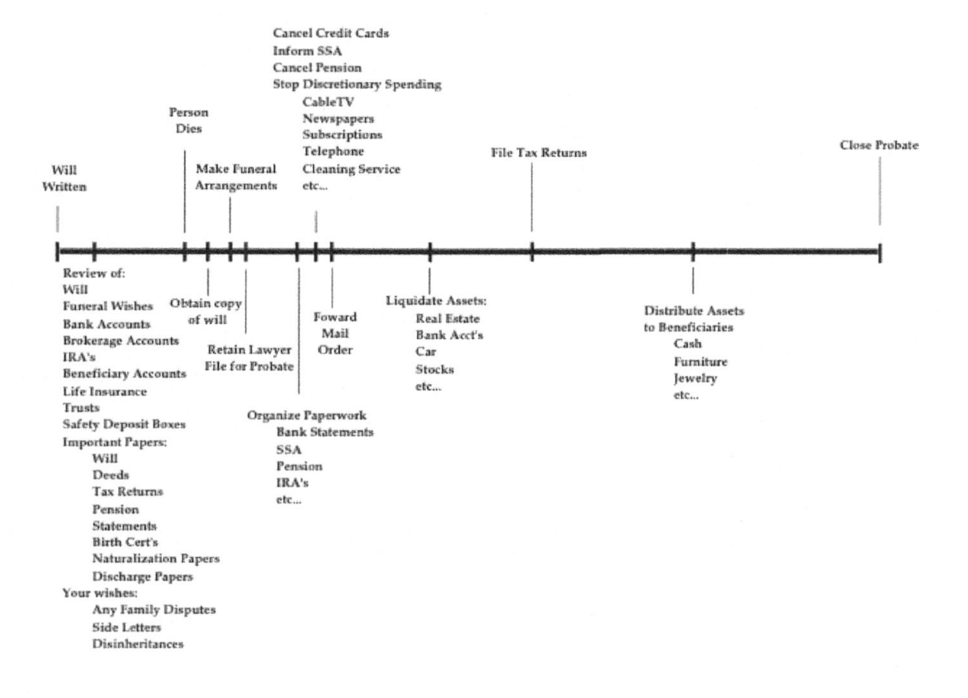

The timeline above is a good indication of when you need to start doing "things." Each is described in more detail in later chapters. You can see that one of the first items in the process is finding out about the person's will before they pass away. If you're an executor, you need to know what to do before your loved one passes away. It makes it easier for everyone. It's also good to know where all the important papers are stored, again, before your loved one passes. They might not want to let you know any of this information because they don't want you to find out how much is in their bank accounts or how many mutual funds they have. That's not what you're looking for. You just want to know where the paperwork is going to be kept, not what's in it, so that you're not scrambling trying to piece together a financial history forensically. That's also how a lot of lost monies are turned over to the state. A small bank account that was forgotten or an overpayment to the insurance company that couldn't be refunded are easily overlooked and can be turned over to the state and not to the beneficiaries if they're not claimed.

You can also see by the above timeline that once the funeral is over, there isn't all that much more to be done—if you're organized. You'll just need to start closing accounts, informing the proper government agencies, transferring stocks, and then distributing funds. It's not all that difficult, and the bulk of the work can absolutely be done without an attorney, saving a significant amount of money in closing out the estate.

So with all that said, make sure that you have a valid original of the will and that you are in fact the executor. You won't officially be the executor until the requisite government authority (probate court in most jurisdictions) says you are but if there is someone else named in the will as the executor you would want to get that out in the open before it goes to probate - why do the work if you're not the one named -or- at least know there is some contention in the process up front.

One important note. If the original will is stapled, do not unstaple it. The reason being is, if the will is challenged an argument can be made that a page was changed and re-inserted and/or there are pages missing. If a copy is to be made, just fold over the stapled pages.

Chapter 2

Remember, No Good Deed Goes Unpunished

Ralph Waldo Emerson once said, "When it comes time to divide an estate,
the politest men quarrel." Keep in mind that no matter how much you want to compromise, make everybody feel good, and make minor accommodations, you are unlikely to please everyone. A thick skin during this time would be your best asset. This is especially true when there is more than one beneficiary. There will be conflicting opinions, different views of what is right and what is wrong, different time schedules, motivations, and so on. It will probably be the case that all the views are a little right and a little wrong. You can't please everyone. You should not try to please anyone. You're going to have competing interests through the entire process, so you'd better get used to it right up front. Just try to do what you think is right, reasonable, equitable, and fair.

You have to do what you think is reasonable or what a reasonable person would do as you administer the estate and "suffer the slings and arrows" of the constituents you serve. In most cases the disputes will be resolved to the satisfaction of most. It's your role to communicate, explain, cajole, ameliorate, and pacify wherever possible. Try to establish a goal that regardless of what happens, there will not be any lasting animosity among the beneficiaries. Don't do things that you think are good—do things that you think are reasonable, equitable, and fair.

One example of not being able to please everyone is in the administration of stock. Since stock has different values at different points in time, those values cannot be predicted with any certainty. Let's say that the stock in the will is worth $1,000 on the date the person dies, January 1, 2020. You have a number of options for the stock's disposal:

1. You can sell the stock, bank the $1,000 in the estate account, and let it earn interest there.

2. You can transfer the stock into the name of the estate, so that the estate owns $1,000 in stock (or just leave it as is until you're ready to transfer it to the beneficiaries).

3. You can transfer the stock directly to the beneficiaries so that they have the benefit of the $1,000.

4. You can sell the stock and hold the cash for the beneficiaries who want the cash and transfer the stock to those who want the shares. In other words, you can sell some of the shares of stock and transfer some of the shares of stock. For example, if there are 2 beneficiaries you can sell half the shares of stock and give the $500 in proceeds to beneficiary 1 and transfer the other half of the shares of stock to beneficiary 2.

You choose option number two and hold on to the stock (through the estate) because you're sure, based on all the market research you've done, that the value of the stock is going to go up. You'll be increasing the value of the estate, which will make everyone happy. You've done a good deed: you're making money for everyone! The unfortunate thing is that you don't know what the future holds.

There are three things that the stock you've held on to can do. It can go up, stay the same, or go down. Let's say that in spite of all the market research you've done, the stock drops in value to $500 by June 1, 2020. The beneficiaries won't be too happy because you could have chosen option one and avoided the loss. Nobody is going to remember that you tried to increase value for them. So your good deed of trying to increase value for the beneficiaries backfired, and you definitely haven't won the hearts and minds of your beneficiaries.

What you could have done is tried to reach a consensus with the beneficiaries as quickly as possible. If a consensus cannot be achieved, distribute the stock right away to each of the beneficiaries. Transfer it into their names. Then they have the option of doing what they want with the stock: either sell or hold. They're responsible, not you. The only time this becomes problematic is if there isn't enough cash money in the estate to pay outstanding bills. So just make sure that if that's the case, you sell the stock and pay off the outstanding bills. The idea is to act reasonably. This book can't list every circumstance that could happen, but if you're reasonable in your approach, you'll have met all your obligations ethically and with integrity.

Chapter 3

Ok, What's Next?

The first statement in some wills says something to the effect that there is a vast amount of uncertainty in this world and that one of the great uncertainties that faces us all is the date, time, and manner of our death. Death could come tomorrow for any one of us. The best thing one can do is be prepared for that inevitability. As the executor, you may not know when you'll be called to do the duty that was entrusted to you. Your loved one can pass suddenly and without any notice. And it may work the opposite way: your loved one may live a long life and pass peacefully in their sleep. Whatever the case, you should be prepared for what's next.

Let's say that your loved one lived a full, productive life and passed away peacefully. You're the executor, and you're wondering what your next steps should be. As noted above, at this immediate point in time, you have the responsibility to carry out your loved one's final wishes and you also have a fiduciary responsibility to the beneficiaries. These wishes were not only entrusted to you informally, through your conversations, but also formally entrusted to you, in front of witnesses, through the writing of a will where you were named as the executor.

As the executor, you're probably going to be making the funeral arrangements. That's the first and most immediate step, and it really can't wait. The funeral is explained in more detail in the next chapter. What you really need to know is that when you are making the arrangements, you need to give input from family and friends the utmost consideration. Decisions are very important.

Once the funeral is over, you are at a key decision point. You'll need to either accept the responsibilities as the executor or relinquish those responsibilities. If you decide to relinquish, someone who is family or a friend can petition the court to allow them to administer the estate. If the court doesn't find them acceptable or there are multiple petitions and an agreement can't be reached, the court may appoint someone for the task. If you have any doubts about your ability to administer the estate, now is the time to petition the court to relieve you of those responsibilities. It is far worse for you and for everyone else involved to get deep into the process and then decide you don't want to serve as the executor. If you want to be relieved, simply write a letter to the probate court explaining that you choose not to accept the responsibility. The court will most likely grant your petition, and at that point, it's out of your hands.

Your other option is to go forward, accept the executor responsibilities, and be named the executor of the will. You should have already gone through the will and have an understanding of your loved one's wishes. You must now execute the instructions contained in the will (and the ones you've received informally) however difficult that is to do. You also need to do it in a comprehensive and responsible manner. Once you have decided to go forward, you'll take a copy of the will, present it to the surrogate court , they will formally name you as the executor (after a period of time), and you will receive from the court what is called a "Letters Testamentary". This "letter" is actually a one-page stamped document that says you are the executor of the estate and can act for your loved one as if they were still alive. In other words, you can sign your name as executor to sell their property, transfer stocks, and so on. This document is very important, and you'll attach it whenever you sign your name to act on the behalf of the estate. Note that you'll need to wait a certain time period before you are named as the executor. Check your state laws or check with your county surrogate court for that time period. Also note that the surrogate court in which you file is typically the county in which your loved one lived. There are exceptions so check with the surrogate court first and they should be glad to help you.

Once you have been confirmed as the executor by the surrogate court and have the Letters Testamentary in hand, you'll make this responsibility as easy as possible for yourself, the family of the deceased, and the beneficiaries if you get ***organized***! As described in the previous chapter, there are things that require your unemotional and immediate attention. *Getting organized* is the best thing you can do for yourself and for the beneficiaries of an estate. How do you get organized? It's not all that complicated, and we'll get to that later.

You will need to pay attention to many, many tasks that need to be accomplished within a few days. There are other tasks and items that you may start now but will take months to finish. You need to be able to focus on those items that require attention in the proper sequence of the process. First things first. You don't want to be focusing on completing the estate tax return while the funeral arrangements need to be made.

The following chapters go into more detail about the steps and the sequence you'll need to follow to close out the estate. Some of this information may seem a little morbid (like describing the nitty-gritty of the funeral details and decisions that you'll need to make) and some is obvious. Ideally, the information will provide you with some guidance on what costs are and how to save on some of them as you move forward.

Chapter 4

The Funeral (Christian)

One of the most emotional parts of this process will be making the funeral arrangements. Making funeral arrangements can also be a cause of great acrimony among siblings. Everyone wants to make sure that her or his opinion is considered. This is also the time that one can be taken advantage of if some preplanning has not been done.

Proper planning and asking questions allow you to make informed decisions. The process will help everyone avoid conflicts as well as avoid making financial decisions based on emotion versus being thought through.

The funeral is where the most decisions probably need to be made. They range from the clothes your loved one will wear to the interior of the casket to the date and time of the funeral and wake. The executor is most likely responsible for making and paying for the funeral arrangements, however, it is not always the case. Someone else may have been tasked with being in charge of the arrangements and the executor and that person should work together on those.

Note that this section is primarily geared towards Christian burial because that is what the authors are most familiar with. The Funeral Director will be able to help with specifics regarding services for any religious denomination or a secular service. Making funeral arrangements consciously or subconsciously sets the tone for the administration of the rest of the estate. If it is done in a participatory but firm and fair manner, taking into consideration everyone's views and opinions before finally making a decision, settling the estate will probably go the same way. If, however, opinions are solicited and each person is given a choice, or one person feels they need to control the process, it will deteriorate into an acrimonious situation very quickly, with bad feelings being the result. That's not a good situation for anyone.

The following paragraphs describe the major items to be considered when planning a funeral.

Selecting a Funeral Home: Remember, funeral homes are in business to sell goods and services and to make a profit, *and there is nothing wrong with that.* That said, you must make sure that you select a reputable funeral home, with people who will discuss all your alternatives and their associated costs as well as payment terms. Just like selecting any other service or product, make sure you get references and ask friends if they have had a positive experience with a particular funeral home. Another starting point is to see if the funeral home is a member of the Order of the Golden Rule.[3] They have and uphold ethical standards for their member funeral homes and have listings of member homes that may help you make a selection. The Better Business Bureau is also a good resource. Check complaint histories and reviews for a funeral home in particular. The Internet is also a resource, but make sure as best as you can that the reviews, positive or negative, are accurate. In New Jersey, all funeral directors must have a

[3] www.ogr.org, a not-for-profit organization

license through the State Board of Mortuary Science. You can view the status of a funeral director's license in New Jersey via the website 'https://newjersey.mylicense.com/verification/' and search for 'Mortuary Science'.

Other states have similar Web-based or call-in methods of checking licensure for funeral home directors.

The key to selecting a funeral home is not to wait until the last minute. There are many circumstances under which a person may pass away. If a hospice organization is involved, they can assist in funeral home selection *before* the person dies. If your loved one is being taken care of by hospice, you should call the funeral home and advise them of the situation. When they pass away, you can call the funeral home and they will come to the house and collect the remains with very minimal intrusion and more dignity than could be afforded by calling 911, the police or EMS.

Finally, when selecting a funeral home pay attention to the geography. For the benefit of the many visitors who may have to travel long distances, select a location that is convenient to the most people who are likely to visit to pay last respects.

Funeral Home Costs: Many elements make up the cost of a funeral. Some are costs incurred directly by the funeral home, such as the rental of the viewing room. Some are "pass-through" costs—those the funeral home pays someone else and for which you pay the funeral home as a matter of convenience. For example, the funeral home may make a donation to the local church or other place of worship for the funeral Mass or service. Funeral homes in New Jersey are required to provide a list of goods and services and their associated costs at the time you are discussing arrangements. Make sure you ask for the list and that you understand what the costs are before booking a funeral.

Let's face it: you have a fiduciary responsibility to act reasonably and a moral obligation to the beneficiaries (however cold it may sound) to get the best-quality funeral at an affordable cost. Consider that any money saved goes directly to the beneficiaries. Those beneficiaries may then put that "saved" money into college funds for their children. There may be no need for a lavish funeral if everyone agrees. If that's the case, everyone can make informed decisions. And maybe the opposite is true: a big funeral with an expensive casket is how everyone wishes to proceed. There is no right or wrong; it's a matter of preference for family and friends. Keep in mind, the funeral is there for the living to ease their grief and to get through the trauma of losing a loved one. With that said, this section is devoted to helping you prepare for the discussion at the funeral home.

See the chart on the next page for the percentage of costs for a funeral home for various expenses.

Funeral Home Percent Costs by Major Expense Items

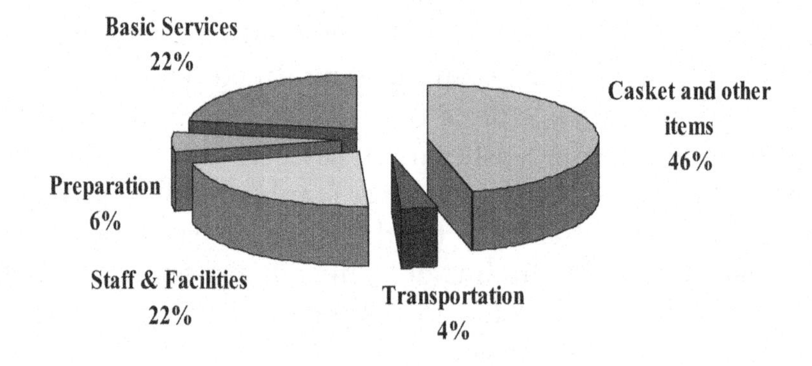

Other typical costs that should be considered are below, along with a recommendation of whether or not to choose them. A summary of the costs is to the right. The cost elements are grouped into their logical categories.

Special COVID-19 note, the Federal Emergency Management Agency (FEMA) has instituted a program to provide financial assistance for funeral expenses for those that qualify. The website is as follows:

https://www.fema.gov/disasters/coronavirus/economic/funeral-assistance

Also note the below was copied directly from the FAQ sections of FEMA.gov website regarding awareness of scams:

"Will FEMA contact me to ask for personal information to register?
FEMA's Funeral Assistance Program has controls in place to mitigate fraudulent activity. **FEMA will not contact anyone until they have called FEMA or have applied for assistance.** Do not disclose information such as the name, birth date or social security number of any deceased family member to any unsolicited telephone calls or e-mails from anyone claiming to be a federal employee or from FEMA.

If you doubt a FEMA representative is legitimate, hang up and report it to the FEMA Helpline at **800-621-3362 or the National Center for Fraud Hotline at 866-720-5721.** Complaints also may be made by contacting local law enforcement agencies."

Basic Funeral Services

◆ *General Services:* These are services done by the funeral director and funeral home staff, and the overhead cost of operating the home. These types of services may include the storage of the decedent's remains, helping to prepare required government documentation, and the paperwork for finance options, overall coordination among all the various parties involved (church, newspaper, and so on), and a general overhead fee.

Preparation of the Body

◆ *Embalming:* There will be a fee for embalming and for an autopsy if one is requested. If there is no legal requirement for an autopsy (there was no criminal involvement and/or the local authorities have not required one), then it is an option that you can choose.

◆ *Makeup:* There will be a charge to apply makeup. The funeral director may require a photo of the deceased so that they can make him or her look as natural as possible. If they don't ask, offer one.

◆ *Hairdresser*: For men and women, there may be a fee for a hairdresser or for a wig.

Funeral Home Staff and Facility

◆ *Wake:* You are renting the funeral home, the services of a funeral director, and assistance and equipment for the duration of the wake. The time period for a wake is whatever you choose. Typically, it is one day with two separate viewings, but again, it can be whatever the family chooses. An option in vogue is one longer viewing versus two separate or having the wake on separate days.

• *Funeral:* You are again renting the funeral home, the services of a funeral director, and assistance and equipment for the duration of the funeral service, including the time at the cemetery.

• *Memorial Service*: You may choose to forgo a wake and funeral service in lieu of a memorial service. A memorial service may take place without the loved ones remains.

Transportation

• *Taking the Remains to the Funeral Home:* This involves taking the body from the place the person died to the funeral home. The funeral director will perform this work, they typically come to the house in a non-descript van and take your loved one out on a stretcher. They will do it with the utmost respect for your loved one. Don't be shocked if there is a body bag as that may be a legal and/or procedural requirement. If your loved one has passed away in another state, there will be procedural (paperwork) items that most likely will delay the process. Again, any reputable funeral director will help streamline the process and act as quickly as possible.

• *Limousine:* This is another option for a funeral. The family can certainly drive themselves. For logistical reasons, this may be more desirable than renting a limousine. For example, if the cemetery is far from the funeral home, you will need to be driven back to pick up your car.

• *Hearse:* There are charges for the hearse, which one may not think about until they show up on the final bill. The funeral home will charge for transporting the body from the place of death (i.e., home or hospital) to the funeral home. The hearse is also used to transport the body from the funeral home to the church, memorial chapel, etc., and then to the cemetery or crematorium.

• *Flower Car(s):* There will be a fee for each provided, however many people today request donations to favorite charities or to the family in lieu of flowers.

Casket and Other Material Items

• *Casket:* The casket is probably the most expensive item in any funeral. Many funeral homes have casket displays with their associated pricing on the premises. You do not need to purchase one from the funeral home. *You can purchase a casket from a casket company*[4] *and have it delivered to the funeral home, and by laws, they cannot refuse it.* Generally the funeral home will offer to match the cost of the casket from a different company (or charge a slightly higher price) for one of their comparable caskets. This may be worthwhile because you can physically see the casket that your loved one will be using. You will also have to select the casket interior. This will generally be included in the price of the casket, but you need to ask the question at the time you are making the selection. One more consideration is casket leasing, especially in the event of a cremation. The funeral home can lease a casket for the viewing and then use another container (generally a cardboard box) for the cremation. This can save on costs, although you definitely want to see the leased casket before you make that decision. You will, however, want to acquiesce to the wishes of the beneficiaries as much as possible. Note

[4]Search the internet for "casket companies"

that waxed cardboard is an option that your state may sanction, this would be for cremation.

- *Urns, Flag Holders, etc.:* This is another personal choice, and you will most likely want to consider the wishes of the beneficiaries, other family, and loved ones. You can purchase these items from the funeral home, from local stores, or on the Internet. They are common items, and you should certainly shop for the style and value you would like.

- *Funeral Cards:* Another item that you may choose to select is funeral cards. These are cards with the loved one's name, date of death, and usually a short passage from scripture, a poem, or some other statement about the person who passed away. They'll come laminated or not; again this is a personal preference, so select them based on style and value.

- *Acknowledgment Cards:* Thank-you cards are customarily sent to people who have donated money, sent flowers, and/or sent Mass cards for the deceased. Make sure that you order enough of these. If you have to order a second run, there may be an additional cost.

- *Flowers:* Flowers should not necessarily be an expense borne by the estate. If the beneficiaries want to send flowers (jointly or individually), they should send them by their own expense. As an executor, you are representing the deceased, and a person wouldn't necessarily send themselves flowers. As noted previously, many choose to note donations to favorite charities or to the family in lieu of flowers.

- *Other Items:* Items such as the guest register book, religious items, and prayer cards are usually offered at nominal cost. It is a good idea to purchase the guest register book so you will have a record of the people who attended the wake or service for your loved one. Since there is only one book, you should make copies of it for all the immediate family members. It will save you some work, because family members may want to send personal thank-you to their friends. Distributing copies of the book to everyone soon after the wake/service will save time down the road.

Pass-through items are those that are coordinated and paid for by the funeral home, at times with a nominal additional fee.

- *Obituary:* Newspapers charge for placing an obituary, and the cost is one that is passed through by the funeral home. It is generally a nominal cost. Keep in mind, though, that each newspaper an obituary is submitted to will have their own charge, so the more newspapers the obituary is sent to, the higher the cost. Most funeral homes have a standard form to complete for submission to the newspaper that includes the age at death, where born, employment, military service, and so on. You do not have to use their form; you can create your own obituary for submission, however, it may result in additional cost depending on the length. **Keep in mind that the obituary serves notice that you are out of the house during the viewing hours and for the funeral.** Make sure that your house is locked and that valuables are stored in a safe place when you are attending services.

- *Pallbearers:* If family and/or friends are not available to be pallbearers, the funeral home will make arrangements to have pallbearers for the casket. There is a cost associated with having the funeral home supply the pallbearers. There may also be a charge for pallbearer gloves. In any event there may be a requirement for pallbearers for the casket. You can have as many as you would like (within reason). The funeral home will make those arrangements and guide you in protocol.

• *Church, Memorial Chapel, Synagogue*: The church will generally require a donation for the funeral service. This is usually a pass-through cost by the funeral home to the church. In addition, a cost not borne by the funeral home is a personal donation to the priest, rabbi or minister for conducting the funeral service.

• *Organist/Pianist:* If the service is being held in a church, an organist or pianist may be required for the music

• *Singer:* This option is a personal preference. If there is a family member or close friend who would like to sing, by all means the church or memorial chapel should accommodate that wish.

• *Accompanist:* Another option based on the wishes of the family.

• *Military Honors:* If the deceased was a veteran, the funeral home will make arrangements to have military funeral honors detail at the funeral ceremony. At a minimum, the honors detail will present a flag, as a tribute for serving their country, flag folding and presentation and taps played. All provided by the United States government at the funeral (or other appropriate time) at no additional cost. Veterans are also eligible by law to have a Medallion and they are available from the Unites States Veterans Administration for placement on private headstones. Have form DD-214 available for the funeral director.

• *Veterans Burial Allowance:* If your loved one was honorably discharged from the military, survivors may be eligible for a burial allowance. Go to va.gov (current link is: 'https://www.va.gov/burials-memorials/veterans-burial-allowance/') to view the criteria.

• *Death Certificate:* The funeral home can provide certified copies of the death certificate, as can the board of health in the municipality in which the person died. It's more convenient to obtain the death certificates at the funeral home. Request the number of copies you'll need all at once, if you know how many you will need in administering the estate. Many states have websites where certified copies of death certificates can be requested online for a fee. Note that you'll need death certificates to sell real property such as the house and cars, to close out the insurance policies, to cancel credit cards, and so on.

• *Cemetery:* There are a number of fees associated with the cemetery. Obviously, there is a cost for the gravesite itself, and the choice of a single, double, or multiple plots. There will be a fee to open the grave. There will be a fee for the type of container or vault for the casket (whether one is necessary depends on the cemetery). Some options are regular unlined concrete vaults, lined (water-resistant) concrete vaults, and bronze, hermetically sealed vaults. This is another one of those personal choices that can be difficult to make. From a purely analytical standpoint, there is not an obvious or logical need for a concrete or any other type of vault. The person will be no less dead and will not feel or know the difference. On the other hand, the family may feel more at ease if they know their loved one is protected from the elements for eternity if they are placed in a hermetically sealed bronze vault. The funeral home will take care of payment to the cemetery as a pass-through cost. Recent options also include "green" burials, which is a choice that the funeral director can explain. They will also be able to explain the rules and regulations for that particular cemetery, for example, many Catholic cemeteries require a Christian symbol on a headstone.

Other Funeral-Associated Items

• *Repast Luncheon:* An estate expense for the traditional (in many parts of the country) after-funeral repast.

• *Headstone*: A headstone may need to be selected. If the person is a veteran, the United States government will provide a small, flat headstone with the person's name, date of birth (DOB), and date of death (DOD) inscribed. There are a number of headstone choices. There are flat or upright stones in granite or marble. Flat markers are also a choice, again in granite, marble, or bronze. The government also provides a bronze niche marker for cremated remains. The funeral home will also make this arrangement for you as part of their service fee. There can be a significant savings if the government provides a headstone. Refer to information from the United States Veterans Administration (the VA). Generally, if the person was on active duty or was discharged honorably, they are entitled to a headstone provided by the VA. See Appendix O for specifics and the form to request a headstone from the VA.

• *Headstone Installation Fee*: This is a fee that is payable directly to the cemetery. The cemetery most likely will require a fee to accept and place the headstone. If a headstone is to be provided by the Veterans Administration, there will be a fee to install the headstone at a private cemetery.

• *Headstone Inscription Fee:* This refers to the fee for carving the person's name, the date of birth, the date of death, and any other inscription on an existing headstone. The cemetery will charge a fee for allowing the firm to do the inscription on the premises. The company that does the carving will also charge their fee to do the actual inscription. Generally, you as the executor will coordinate this activity as part of the funeral arrangements; however, you are not required to do so. This is one of the items that fall outside the bounds of the estate. Each of the *next of kin* must be in agreement with what is placed on the headstone. Each of the next of kin has an interest in the cemetery plot where the person is to be buried. You may run into a situation where there is disagreement over the headstone inscription. For example, assume there are four beneficiaries for an estate and assume they are all children of the deceased, next of kin. All are in agreement that the DOB and DOD of the deceased should be on the headstone; however, there is a disagreement about the inscription. Two of the next of kin want an inscription that the other two do not. If all parties can't reach agreement, the cemetery will not allow any inscription. In fact, an affidavit needs to be signed by all the living next of kin to have the inscription done.

These are the typical expenses you can expect when planning a funeral. As noted above, the assumption is that you are a beneficiary, a next of kin, and the executor of the estate, so you will have those responsibilities concurrently. If you are not one of the next of kin, you'll be responsible for paying for reasonable funeral expenses from the estate.

Chapter 5

Get Organized!

Now that the funeral is over, and if you have not already done so, it is time to get organized. You will need to go through your loved ones files, contact various state and government agencies, hire a lawyer, take care of mundane day-to-day items, sell parts of the estate, distribute stock, close accounts. . . . The list goes on and on. Think of it as running another household in its entirety. If you can't get organized and follow a logical sequence of events, you'll struggle to administer the estate. More important, you may incur additional costs in the administration.

Setup: Create a system, one that works for you. A recommendation to get organized would be to devote some space in your house/apartment solely to the estate. Set aside a shelf, desk space, a room, or a filing cabinet. In that space keep only the items that relate to the estate. Next, get a filing cabinet and/or folder in which to keep the various estate documents in an organized manner. It goes without saying that you should categorize each document and keep them in alphabetical order. Get a notebook where you can document various items. Set aside some space for estate receipts. We have provided Word and Excel templates (see appendices) that you can use to help keep track of the estate information. They are also online at www.executorbook.com, see the templates tab and the password is 'thebook' (without quotes).

The next step is to go through all the decedent's paperwork. Separate all the paperwork into logical categories of assets and liabilities.

Estate assets include items such as the following:

- Account statements
- Bank statements (checking, savings, CDs)
- Brokerage statements
- Transfer agents (stocks held)
- Stock certificates
- Fund statements (mutual funds, bonds, AMEX, etc.)
- Retirement (401k, IRA, company plan)[5]
- Social Security statement[6]
- Pay statements
- Title to cars, boats, airplanes
- Insurance statements

---

[5]Not part of the estate, but there is an executor responsibility here that is discussed in later chapters.

[6] Create an online account if one does not already exist at 'www.ssa.gov'

    - House
    - Personal catastrophe
    - Boat, plane, etc.
- House (or any other real estate)
- Deeds
- Life insurance[7]
- Warrantees
- Mortgage or mortgage satisfaction document
- Any real property
- Jewelry
- Furnishings
- Coin Collection(s)

Estate liabilities are items such as the following:

- Household expenses, bills
- Gas bill, electric bill, cable TV bill
- Phone bill

---

[7] Another item typically that passes outside the estate

- Medical bills
- Professional fees
- Lawyer
- Accountant
- Misc. estate expenses
- Tax returns from previous five years (or more)

Make a folder for each one of the above categories, arrange the statements by date, and just file the folders until you're ready to go.

Document, Document, Document! When it comes to documentation, you can't have enough. You may have to show the IRS these records. Document everything you do for the estate. Keep track of your phone calls in a phone log and/or keep the phone bill, your mileage in a mileage log, and the time you spend working on estate matters in another separate log. Make sure that you record the date, start and stop times, and a brief description of what you were working on. Appendix R contains templates for mileage and time logs.

Schedule: You may want to work on the estate only during predefined time periods and determine how much you will work on the estate in a given day. The administration of an estate is like running a small business but has the added pressure of dealing with bereavement, grief, and all other types of emotional stress. The recommendation is to work on the estate on an unemotional level as best as possible and in that vein, schedule the time you spend wisely.

You'll work on the estate each and every day in the beginning. If you don't set aside a small amount of time each day to pay bills, review statements, and do other estate work, you will find yourself far behind when it comes time to provide the beneficiaries or attorney with basic estate information. That said, there is typically no hard and fast deadline to close the estate, however, it goes back to your fiduciary responsibility to the beneficiaries. If you delay and it causes harm you could face some form of penalty or petition to be removed.

Scheduling time to work on the estate is just another way to ensure that you are organized and on top of the administration process.

Chapter 6

Your Lawyer

Why do you need a lawyer? The answer is, you don't. You can file all the paperwork yourself, such as the will (in probate court), refunding bonds, limit to creditors, and other legal forms and paperwork. You can have the court issue you the letters testamentary, which allows you to act on behalf of the estate. You can open bank accounts and stock accounts in the name of the estate. Each of those items is simple to do and does not require the services of an attorney. The problem, however, is that you may make a mistake in filing or miss a deadline because you were not aware of the filing requirements for certain documents. If you make such an error in the administration of the estate, you can and will be held liable. This is true whether you have a lawyer or not. That being the case, why have a lawyer at all? Two reasons: first, the lawyer will be knowledgeable about the court process in closing an estate, and second, your lawyer will help prevent you from making mistakes.

The recommendation is that you hire a lawyer, hold an overview meeting with him or her. Let your lawyer know that you will do all the account closings, filings, and so on, with the lawyer acting as a double check and of course, listen to the advice they offer on that. They may believe that the estate is too large and/or complex for the uninitiated to handle or that it would not be in your/the estates best interest to proceed that way.

You must also be careful in the selection of a lawyer. Too many times the lawyer is selected only because he or she wrote the will or is a friend of the family, or because you may be related to one. *Please do not make this the selection criteria.* Selecting a lawyer to represent the estate (and hence, you as the estate representative) is one of the most important decisions you will make as you go through the administration process. Done correctly, it will likely save money as you close probate. Done incorrectly, it will cause you more anxiety and incur more cost than you could have ever been prepared for.

You need to start the selection process by understanding one fundamental and overarching premise: the lawyer is there to provide you with *advice and counsel.* In fact, a lawyer is defined as "One whose profession is to give legal advice and assistance to clients and represent them in court or in other legal matters."[8] The lawyer is not responsible for making decisions about the estate; *you are.*

The lawyer *is* responsible for providing you with expertise, skill, and legal advice for matters of estate administration. A lawyer should also provide you with some practical advice based on their experience with estates. It is important for you to remember that you are "purchasing" their skill and expertise and are a customer, just as if you were a customer purchasing the skill of any other professional. One thing to guard against, however, is having the relationship between you and the lawyer become one of customer/supplier. You

[8]http://www.dictionary.com

want the lawyer to provide a pragmatic approach to issues that arise, to work with you on reducing costs, and to help you with the beneficiaries (and/or their lawyers) as questions from them come up. Simply stated, you want the relationship to be one of partnership, gaining agreement and setting expectations up front and then using that as a basis for going forward with the administration of the estate.

Because you are responsible for decisions about the estate and the lawyer is there only to provide advice, you can and should provide direction to the lawyer. For example, if you want the estate funds deposited in a certain bank and not the lawyer's trust fund, you are fully within your rights to insist upon that. The lawyer will advise you about the legal (and ideally, practical) ramifications of that decision, but, as noted above, it is your decision to make. If you want to use your own bank and not use the lawyer's trust fund at all, that is fair game also.

The lawyer may also be useful because if there is an error made in the estate administration, they will generally be held liable for it. For example, if a creditor surfaces after the estate is closed and the proper documents were not filed with the court, the lawyer can potentially be held liable and ordered to pay that creditor. The same holds true for filing papers incorrectly (or not in a timely manner) with the court. The lawyer is responsible for those legal devices. If they say they will file papers in a timely and appropriate manner and they don't, they may be legally liable.
The criteria that should be used to select an attorney are as follows: They should have their practice within the county in which the person died. This can be helpful if items need to be expedited or the court has questions. It also helps if the lawyer

has a general familiarity with the way the surrogate court works within that particular county.

You can seek a lawyer who is a family member, friend of the family, or personal friend. You just need to make sure that the relationship you have with the lawyer you select does not leave the estate (and you) open to a potential conflict of interest or hint at impropriety. For example, the beneficiaries may ask questions such as why the fee is so high, why some decisions seem to favor one person more than another, why it seems as if there is a conflict. It might just not be worth the aggravation. Another consideration is the firing process. There may come a time when you want to fire the lawyer. If your lawyer were a personal friend, would you be able to fire him or her if you thought you weren't getting good advice, or they were unresponsive to your queries? It comes down to how comfortable you are with the lawyer and making sure there is no conflict. The lawyer can actually help you determine that during the initial meeting you have with him or her.

The first place to start your selection process for a lawyer is through friends and acquaintances. Some may be able to recommend a lawyer who has handled estates as their area of expertise. *You must hire a lawyer whose practice specialty is probate.* Just as you wouldn't go to a cardiologist to set a broken leg, you should not go to a trial lawyer to handle an estate. You want the experience and contacts that go with the estate specialty for that practice. Another good place for lawyer recommendations is the American Bar Association (ABA). The ABA will recommend lawyers in your area with an estate practice. They will not, however, comment on their skill. You can do somewhat of a background check through the Martindale Hubble website (see Appendix B). This website may give some type of background information on the attorney—at a minimum the law school attended, and the year admitted to the bar. Martindale also can give you some recommendations. Your state and local bar associations are also good places to get recommendations for lawyers who specialize in probate. And the obvious, look online for any and all reviews for a particular lawyer and law firm.

Once you have a number of recommendations, we strongly advise that you interview a minimum of two if not three of those lawyers. This will give you a good feel for their fee schedule, their experience, the way the office is run, the chemistry between you, and other indications of how well you will interact.

You do not want a lawyer who

- appears to have a heavy caseload,
- does not seem enthusiastic or genuinely interested,
- is not personable,
- is selling his or her services too aggressively,
- does not understand the relationship you have in mind (partners—but you are the boss),
- has issues with online reviews
- has a conflict of interest, or
- has complaints filed against him or her with the American Bar Association.

In summary, you need to hire a lawyer with whom you feel comfortable, who has experience with estates and wills, and whose services you can purchase at a reasonable cost.

One of the most important questions after you have gone through the interview process is about the law firms' fee schedules. You'll want to find out how much the legal services will cost, what the cost drivers are, and when the estate will be billed for those services.

Most law firms will charge you an hourly rate for estate administration. Those fees vary widely among firms, so it is wise to do a comparison. You should also ask how those fees are billed. Many firms bill in six-minute increments. If their hourly rate is $200 per hour, you will be charged approximately $33 every six minutes. You should be aware of the cost considerations when you are interacting with your lawyer in person, via telephone, or via written correspondence. One item to be aware of is that written correspondence with the lawyer can actually drive up your costs. You might think that you're going to save money by writing instead of speaking with the lawyer, but that is not necessarily the case. Every time you copy the lawyer on a letter, it is billable time. The reason it's billable is that the lawyer will review it for any issues or problems that it may cause the estate. The object lesson is not to copy the lawyer on mundane items and also to batch correspondence. For example, if the lawyer is holding estate funds in an escrow account, you will need to request checks from the them to pay various household bills such as gas, electric, taxes, and insurance (assuming that there is a house involved). Rather than sending a letter to the lawyer requesting a check as each bill comes due, send a letter once or twice per month and request a number of checks at the same time. Do the same for all deposits, such as refund checks or stock dividends that need to be made. Submit those to the lawyer once or twice per month to help save some of the administrative cost.

So what will the lawyer typically do for you? They will represent you in the administration of the estate with any interested parties such as the court, creditors, insurance companies, and other people or entities who may come into contact with the estate. They will provide consultation in person or by phone, let you know how the process is progressing, provide legal and practical advice, and review documents pertaining to the estate. If you choose, they will also prepare and file any tax returns for the estate.

All of the above information should be documented in a retainer agreement that both you and the lawyer sign. It is the basis for "who does what" in the administration of the estate. The fee schedule needs to be documented here, as do the items that will be billable.

After you have selected a lawyer and signed the retainer agreement, the two of you should have a formal meeting. You should spend some time preparing for this meeting so it will be as productive as possible for both you and the lawyer. Listed here are some of the items you should locate and make copies of before the meeting:

- Previous-year tax returns
- Bills (e.g., utility, insurance)

- List of (large) physical assets such as
    - home
    - property
    - car(s)
    - boat(s)
- Bank account statements
- Certificates of Deposit (CD) statements
- Safety deposit box information
- Brokerage firm statements (Stocks)
- IRAs
- 401k
- Life insurance

At this initial meeting, you and the lawyer will review each of these items and develop a plan for how each of the accounts and assets will be handled and by whom. You may want the lawyer to handle any and all transactions. You may decide to close all the bank accounts and allow the lawyer to handle the transfer of securities. You may decide to do all the work with the exception of dealing with probate court. Whatever you decide, now is the time to have a clear understanding between you and your lawyer.

Selecting a lawyer is one of the most important things you can do for the administration of an estate. Make sure you select from a number of lawyers, interview them, check their backgrounds, and work with them in partnership while maintaining the role of client.

Chapter 7

Paperwork You Can File Yourself

Below is a list of steps that need to be taken and paperwork that needs to be filed. You can file these items yourself, have your lawyer file them, or a combination of both.

- *Probate the Will:* This refers to filing the will with the surrogate court. Probate is simply the legal process that establishes the genuineness of the will. Generally, a will is probated in the state and county where the person resided at the time of his or her death. The lawyer will simply assist you in filing the will with the county surrogate, although you can do it yourself. Call your county surrogate and ask to make an appointment to file the will. The surrogate's office will most likely provide you with any and all assistance you need and guide you individually through the probate process. It's important to note that in most states, there is a waiting period between the time your loved one dies and when you can present the will to probate court. That time period is usually ten calendar days.

- *Notice to Beneficiaries:* You also must notify the next of kin, the surviving spouse, and all beneficiaries in writing within a certain time period that begins when the will has been probated. This allows those people to challenge the will if they so choose. Your or your lawyer will then file a notice with the probate court within the prescribed time period after that notice is given. See Appendix A for a sample letter. Make sure you send the letter via postal certified mail, return receipt requested, and save the return receipt. Depending on the state where the will has been filed, you will need to inform the surrogate court that the notice to beneficiaries has been sent. You'll also need to provide an affidavit or other evidence that the notice has been given. The return receipt from the post office will suffice.

- *Notice to Interested Parties:* Some states require you to notify specific people who are not beneficiaries but would have an interest in the will. Usually those people are a spouse and children of the deceased who are not named as beneficiaries for some reason. If you have any questions, just ask the surrogate's office and they'll be glad to let you know who actually needs to be informed. The notice to interested parties also has specific time frames for sending those letters.

- *Tax Identification Number (tax ID):* You'll need to file IRS form SS-4 to obtain a tax ID number for the estate. It is also called an Employer Identification Number (EIN). This is important because some brokerages and banks require a tax ID number before they will close any accounts in the estate name. Also, some states require that the tax ID number be used when income taxes are filed. The Internal Revenue Service allows the form to be completed online at *https://irs.usa-*

taxid.com/products/EINEstate. We highly recommend completing the form online. The IRS website offers a step-by-step approach, but a copy of the actual form is in Appendix X.

- *Tax Returns, Federal and State:* These too are must-file forms. The tax return is completed almost as if the deceased were filing it themselves. For example, Form 1040 (or 1040A) is used, and standard deductions apply, as do filing deadlines. If you're comfortable and knowledgeable with this process, you can certainly complete the tax return for the estate. There are a number of tax software packages on the market that make it easy to file. You can also hire an accountant or accounting firm.

- *Open Estate Checking Account:* One very important item to remember is to *never commingle estate funds with personal funds.* You want to keep those monies separate. The reason is that you have control of the estate funds, you have the physical checks that are in the estate's name, and you'll be making deposits into the estate account. You need to be able to account for all the money in the estate. If you commingle funds, it will be difficult, if not impossible, to determine to whom the money belongs. As noted in other sections, the estate checking account should be in your name as executor and be interest bearing (if practicable). If you have a lawyer open the estate account, you need to require him or her to provide you with monthly bank statements for all account transactions and balances so that you can verify the account balance.

- *Out-of-State Transactions and Forms:* This step applies in a limited number of cases where, for example, there is a vacation home out of state. We recommend that you have an attorney help with this even if you live in a state that does not require an attorney to close on property.

- *Order to Limit Creditors:* This is something you request from the surrogate court, which issues the order. It says that any creditor has a certain time period, usually six months, to make a claim against the estate. This is a critical filing for two reasons:

    - If the order is not in place, a creditor can make a claim against the estate years later and all beneficiaries may have to pay that claim even if the estate is closed.

    - It allows you to know what the estate liabilities are without going through a protracted amount of time.

  To implement the order, work with your local surrogate's office and they will help guide you through the process.

- *Refunding Bond and Release:* Before any of the estate proceeds are distributed, all beneficiaries must sign a Refunding Bond and receive a completed copy. This is another very important document, because if there are any unforeseen circumstances where just debts are owed, the beneficiaries are agreeing to refund money distributed by the estate to satisfy that debt. This means that if the government is still owed money after the estate is closed, that money can be collected from the beneficiaries as if the estate had not been closed out. Refunding bonds are filed with the surrogate court. That ensures that if a beneficiary does not refund money owed, there is a court record saying that they agreed to do it, and that beneficiary can be compelled to pay their fair share. The release discharges the executor from their duty as an executor once the estate has been distributed to the beneficiaries. It shows that the executor is no longer responsible for the estate and that the obligation to the estate has been fulfilled.

- *Final Accounting:* This is a record of all money and property in the estate, as well as money paid out and taken in by the estate and includes disbursement to the beneficiaries. The final accounting shows the monetary value of the estate when your loved one passed, how much was paid out in debts (i.e., credit card bills, taxes,) how much came in from items such as insurance refunds, and what was left over for the beneficiaries. There are different requirements, depending on the state in which the will was probated. Some states allow for an informal final accounting where you simply report the aggregate totals for value that existed, value that went out, value that came in, and the monetary amount distributed to the beneficiaries. Some states will allow the signing of the Refunding Bond and Release as the de-facto final accounting. Many states have the forms you will need on their websites. The final accounting accompanies the refunding bonds when you make distributions to beneficiaries.

As the executor, you can file all the forms above without assistance. This book provides sample forms in the appendices that you can use in most states with some slight modifications. If you need specific information for your state, you can usually find it on the state website and download the appropriate forms there.

It's important to know that there are different types of beneficiaries and their classifications and vary by state. For example in New Jersey, children (biological and adopted) of the deceased are called Class A beneficiaries. Siblings (again biological and adopted) are Class B and so on as the relation moves further away from the deceased. There are also classes where there is no familial relation. The different types of classes each come with different implications regarding taxes. As the executor just be familiar with the classes and be aware that taxes will be paid by the beneficiary based on their Beneficiary Class. In some states, there are also people who are entitled to a percentage of the estate even if they are not listed as beneficiaries in the will or are even specifically excluded. Your local surrogate will be able to help with the applicable state laws.

Chapter 8

Dealing with Siblings, Relatives, and Friends

There are a few indisputable facts when you deal with people close to you as you administer the estate: everybody will have an opinion, each opinion will be different, and you will receive advice from everyone, some of it good and some of it bad. You will need the ability to listen to those opinions impartially and discern the good advice from the bad and have the fortitude to do what you think is right and reasonable. You'll need to do all these things while making sure they don't consume all of your time, because they certainly can if you let them. Just be guided by what the will provides for, doing what you think is right and how you think a reasonable person would act in a similar situation, and you won't have to worry about a thing.

Dealing with Siblings: In the majority of cases, the executor of the estate is a son or daughter with one or more siblings, and they are all equal beneficiaries. They will all believe they have an equal voice in how the estate should be administered and most likely will have strong recommendations along those lines. Although you need to listen to those opinions because some may have value, you still need to make your own decisions and not acquiesce to theirs if they are unreasonable. Don't make decisions that are based on "keeping the peace" if there is not a 'win/win' in that decision. Poor decisions made solely to placate one sibling satisfy no one and make things worse, because they are inherently viewed as showing favoritism to oneself or another sibling.

Siblings have a unique kind of a bond because they share a common childhood and know each other's strengths and weaknesses very well, and each had a parent/child bond with the decedent. Those relationships can allow an emotional decision-making process to come into play. If you make a decision with which a sibling doesn't agree, they will probably suggest that "Mom/Dad didn't want it that way" or "Mom/Dad would not have agreed with that" or other similar thoughts along those lines. That may be a large emotional hurdle you need to overcome, but you need to put it aside and make decisions based on the facts of the situation, whatever they may be. To counter such statements, you can gently remind your siblings that Mom/Dad didn't have all the facts at hand, and what they thought while they were alive no longer fits the situation as it is today. That is a less antagonistic way of dealing with siblings. It might prevent an emotional viewpoint from working its way into an otherwise rational decision-making process.

Siblings and/or beneficiaries will most likely have spouses. Those spouses will have their own opinions as well, and those opinions may become another point of contention in the overall process. They will have some degree of influence over the way the siblings/beneficiaries react to your administration of the estate. They may feel that you are not looking out for their best interests—or worse, they may feel you are making decisions to the detriment of their spouse. In some instances, that may appear to be the case. You may make a decision that is not in the best interests of a particular person but is in the best interests of the estate. That's the job of the executor: to do what is best for the estate, not an individual.

Another interesting phenomenon occurs among siblings when the last parent passes away, especially if the last parent is the mother. It may be difficult to accomplish certain, seemingly mundane tasks because one sibling perceives them as being cold and unfeeling or think "the time is just not right." For example, having the phone disconnected may evoke feelings against the executor because "that was moms number" which equates to an allegory of severing contact with mom. It may be because the phone number is associated with the parent and disconnecting the number is further reinforcement that the parent is dead and not coming back. The same can happen with the sale of the house, car, clothing, or anything else that may have been of significance to the parent. As a matter of practicality, the phone has to be disconnected, the house sold, and the clothing distributed or sold.

One other area that can be a point of contention is deciding which beneficiary keeps which personal, sentimental item from the parent. These personal and sentimental items can range from the very expensive (an engagement ring) to those of little value (a $1.50 knickknack brought back from a vacation). In later chapters we recommend an approach to dividing such items. The point in this chapter is that as the executor, you must firmly assert, and make sure the beneficiaries clearly understand, that those items are part of the estate and do not belong to any one beneficiary (assuming nothing is explicitly stated in the will, of course). It is not appropriate for one sibling to say that a particular item is theirs (hence not included in the estate) for any reason *unless it is explicitly stated in the will or in a codicil.* For example, jewelry does not belong to a daughter nor do tools belong to a son. Those items belong to the estate and should be distributed accordingly. It works the same way with gifts, if a child gave mom a particular gift for her birthday, that "gift" belongs to the estate, not to that child. It's not always all black and white, however. If the person who passed wrote a list of who gets what, it might not be legally binding, but from an ethical and moral perspective, those items probably should be distributed along those lines.

Relatives: The relatives will probably react in much the same way as siblings. They may feel that they were very close to the person who passed away, and rightly so. This becomes an issue only when they feel close and therefore believe they are entitled to interfere with the affairs of the estate or even with the funeral arrangements. A brother or sister of the deceased or maybe a niece or nephew won't agree with or appreciate what you're doing. They also may feel that they are entitled to something from the estate. A niece may want the picture back she gave to the person who passed. It might be a piece of jewelry. In any event, if gifts were given, they belonged to the deceased and are part of the estate, just as noted above if a child gave a parent a gift. In that type of situation it might be worthwhile, however, to give that relative that gift back if all the beneficiaries agree. The overall monetary value may be small while the comparative overall good will that could be lost great.

As with siblings, you need to strike a balance between the proper administration of the estate and alienating a dear family member who simply wants to help. If the parent has passed away, that parent may have discussed funeral wishes with a brother or sister, not wanting to burden his or her children with that information (assuming the executor is a child and responsible for making the funeral arrangements). In this instance, the input should be more than welcomed; in fact, it should be encouraged.

The issue arises when the relative decides to bypass constructive advice and interfere with administration. This can take the form of nuisance calls and/or correspondence to you or siblings. Even this can be overlooked, and to keep harmony within the family, you the executor can put any acrimony aside. This type of influence, although meddlesome, will probably cease once the passage of time dulls the grief of losing a loved one. What can't be overlooked is a relation who is making unwelcome or irrational demands upon you.

These irrational demands may take the form of wanting items from the estate because they feel a sense of ownership based on the nature of their relationship with the deceased. For example, assume the person who has died inherited furniture from a parent. A sibling may feel that because a common parent owned it, it belongs to them and not to the estate. This is a situation where diplomatic skills need to come into play to firmly remind the relative that items belonging to the deceased are now part of the estate.

You have some options in this situation, however. Among beneficiaries, you may decide to give that furniture to the relative in order to maintain the familial bonds. You may decide to sell the furniture to the relative after discussion with the beneficiaries. You may also tell that relative that the furniture will remain as part of the estate and that you won't entertain any other discussion.

If agreement can't be reached, the relation may decide to challenge the estate in court. Don't take it personally; work with your lawyer to decide the best way to meet that challenge.

The key point to remember is that relatives may make unreasonable demands of you. These demands are most likely rooted in a sense of grief and loss and are not malicious in nature. It may be that they need a sense of control which comes from a situation where there couldn't be any control. However, they may be a result of just the opposite. From a personal standpoint, you need to sort these out and always keep in mind that you have been entrusted by the deceased with a fiduciary relationship to the estate, hence to the beneficiaries. If you have to make a decision that could go either way, you should fall on the side of the person who gave you the responsibility for administering the estate and make a decision favorable to the estate.

Friends: There are only three things to remember here. Your friends will

- have advice,
- share their opinions, and
- tell you you're getting screwed.

Of course, you want to listen to the advice and opinions of your friends. They may have valuable suggestions from their own experiences that can make the process easier and faster. They may have worked with a professional whom they would highly recommend. It's to your advantage not to discount any of that advice or any of those opinions. The comments that may not be productive are the ones where they think you're getting screwed.

Just don't fall into the trap of allowing your friends to guide your thought process through the administration.

Chapter 9

Dealing with Your Spouse or Partner

Depending on how long you've been together and their relationship with the deceased, your spouse or partner will invariably have input into how you are closing the estate. They may want certain things of sentimental value from the estate. They might think the other beneficiaries are taking advantage of you. They also may just want to help you in any way possible in closing the estate so your family life can get back to normal.

Your best course of action may be not to get them involved. You can use this chapter to help soften the blow; you might let them read it for themselves to help them understand the reasons why you're not getting them involved.

The reason you don't want them to be involved is that they will look at the situation emotionally and with partiality. Your job is to be unemotional and impartial for the beneficiaries - remember fiduciary responsibility. For the sake of argument, let's say that your spouse/partner can look at the situation unemotionally and impartially.

The money and the other items from the estate are not theirs. They belong to the beneficiaries. To have not only the beneficiaries, but also the added burden of the rest of the group sitting around the room saying "I want" only serves to complicate matters. This is true even if everyone in the beneficiary group is a family member or the group vacations together. The opinions that come out of having a spouse involved serve no purpose. They will look out for your best interests, which is commendable, but that isn't part of your job as executor.

We are certainly not recommending that the executor keep the spouse/partner in the dark. Far from it. The advice and counsel that you receive from your trusted partner helps keep you on balance and see things you might have missed and will also help to serve as a safety valve when you need someone to speak with. There will be many times throughout the process when you think you're being taken advantage of, or you'll be frustrated in general with the way things are going. Remember, the beneficiaries are looking out for themselves and their interests. This is not a malicious statement; it is more of a pragmatic viewpoint.

Chapter 10

What About You?

You are going to spend a lot of time doing things you need to do as an executor. The people you are doing them for (namely the beneficiaries) will most likely not appreciate the work required of you, because they can't understand the time and effort it takes to administer the estate. The attorney will appreciate you in the sense that you're a customer. Same with the realtor and the accountant. You are a customer. The reminder is that these folks are not there for emotional support, they are providing a service for you and the estate and try to lean on them for their past experience and expertise not as someone to complain to.

You probably work to earn a living. When you do a good job, it's certainly recognized by your peers and ideally by your boss. If you do an exemplary job, that recognition will probably manifest itself in "pats on the back" by peers and (ideally) monetarily by your boss. Do not count on any such recognition while you are administering the estate. In fact, count on sniping and pettiness, and get used to the feeling that no one really cares about the job you're doing or how it may affect your personal life.

It is very difficult, if not impossible, to satisfy all the needs of the beneficiaries. At times, you may make reasonable decisions that are diametrically opposed to the decisions the beneficiaries want you to make. Take the sale of the house, for instance. As the executor you will probably want to sell the house quickly, especially if it is vacant. One of the beneficiaries might want you to delay the sale of the house because they live out of state and are used to using it as a "home base" to visit friends in the area. Another beneficiary might want you to delay because there is an emotional attachment and they don't want to let go, i.e., they visited their mom at the house every other day for tea. And yet another beneficiary might want to have the house sold quickly so the estate closes faster because they are financially strapped and need the money.

The point of the preceding paragraph is that with all the differing points of view and motivations, it is difficult if not impossible to accommodate everyone's needs. Therefore, don't try. For your own well-being and to minimize issues later, you must act as a reasonable person would, and should justify and explain the logic of your every decision. A great American statesman once said, "If you do the right thing, you will never have anything to worry about." This is one of those cases.

Your Expenses: The estate should reimburse you for any out-of-pocket expenses you incur on behalf of the estate. We strongly advise you to keep these to a minimum. For example, don't pay utility bills from your checking account; have an estate check issued. There will be times, though, that having estate-issued checks is just not practical. For example, when mailing paperwork in to transfer securities, you'll use certified mail. It wouldn't be practical to determine the certified mail cost, get a check, and then have to explain to the postal clerk why an estate check for $4.52 will be forthcoming made out to the U.S.

Postal Service. Pay these small expenses via cash or personal check, obtain a receipt, and request reimbursement on a monthly basis from the estate account.

Also, keep track of your mileage if you're driving on behalf of the estate. For instance, when you check on the house, travel to meetings with the lawyer or surrogate court, or drive to perform any other estate-related task, you should be reimbursed for that mileage expense. The lawyer should be able to help you out with a per-mile charge for the estate. What you need to do is keep a diary that lists the date of each trip, the number of miles driven, and the reason for the trip; you'll use it when you submit a claim to the estate for your mileage.

The Executor Fee: Generally, the executor is entitled to a reasonable fee from the estate for the services provided. In many states, this fee is a percentage of the estate. In New Jersey, it's 5 percent for the first $200,000 and 2.5 percent for the remainder. If the estate's total value is $650,000, the fee to the executor would be $21,250, free from taxes. That is not an insubstantial amount. You must remember, however, that you will be putting in extraordinary time and effort administering the estate, and you deserve to be compensated for that.

Your first inclination may be to waive the executor fee, especially if the loved one was a parent and all the beneficiaries are siblings. We strongly recommend that you ***not*** *waive your right to be compensated for the administration of the estate.* You can decide whether or not to collect the fee when the estate is ready to close. There are many reasons that you may change your position about collecting the executor fee. The beneficiaries may generate additional work for you during the year or two when you are administering the estate. Based on that, you should be fairly compensated for your time. You might need the leverage of collecting the fee to counter some irrational claim or position one of the beneficiaries takes when property is divided. For example, a beneficiary might want to keep a $10,000 engagement ring and not make that equitable for the other beneficiaries. If you keep your right to the fee, you can use it as leverage to counter that strategy or at least make everyone else whole (equitable) after the estate is closed.

Whether to keep the fee is a personal decision and one that needs to be made logically and unemotionally. You can rationalize keeping the fee or not keeping the fee many different ways. One might use the rationale that the loved one did not understand that the executor is due such a large fee and that keeping the fee would cause an inequity and therefore shouldn't be kept. One might rationalize that because of the time, energy, and skill expended, the executor fee was more than earned. One can make a case for both scenarios, and this is one of those decisions that must be made personally. If one of your objectives is to assure that the family ties are not broken by this death and that no irreparable harm is done to the relationships among the siblings, then you must seriously consider not taking the fee. As stressed above, this decision must be made logically, not in haste, and with the overarching test being reasonableness. Most states will also not allow the executor (if challenged) to keep an entire executor fee for closing a simple estate. For example, let's say that the estate is worth $500,000, all in a single mutual fund. There is no house or car or furniture, and there is only a minimal amount of jewelry. The actual amount of time to close the estate by selling the mutual fund and distributing the jewelry was about five hours. A minimal amount of time was invested for distribution of a large sum. In some states the fee may be as high as $15,000 to $20,000. If the executor chooses to take the fee, the beneficiaries can challenge that in court as unreasonable or unjust enrichment. You would need to check state law or with an attorney to determine if that's the case. It goes back to reasonableness. It may be viewed as unreasonable to take $20,000 from the estate for 5 hour's worth of work.

Another consideration is treating the administration of the estate as separate from your personal life. For example, don't get caught up in answering questions from the beneficiaries at night and on weekends on a regular ongoing basis. You'll be doing enough work on the estate as it is, and by keeping the "after-hours" calls and queries from the beneficiaries, lawyer, or real-estate agent to a minimum, you'll be doing yourself a favor. As with any job, there will be times when you'll need to interact with the other professionals you've hired at night and on weekends, but they will also want to keep that to a minimum.

You could establish ground rules up front with the beneficiaries and let them know politely but firmly that you won't entertain calls at night or on weekends about the estate except on an emergency basis. They also need to know not to call you at your place of business, because that may become disruptive. There are a number of techniques you can use to keep the beneficiaries in the loop while keeping direct interaction to a minimum. You can schedule monthly status meetings, send letters on a regular schedule or communicate via e-mail. You are usually under no obligation, however, to keep the beneficiaries informed about the administration of the estate. It is simply prudent to do so.

Chapter 11

The Money

It might seem counterintuitive, but this is the easy part. One of your responsibilities as an executor is to pay the bills and to collect money owed to the estate. You or your lawyer will have opened an estate checking account at a bank (remember to use the tax ID number from Chapter 7—Paperwork You Can File Yourself"), which is insured by the Federal Deposit Insurance Corporation (FDIC) up to a specified amount. There are some nuances to FDIC insured accounts so check their website if there is any question. The account should also be interest bearing; many banks today offer free checking with interest as long as a minimum (usually $500 or $1,000) balance is maintained. Your lawyer will probably recommend that they keep the checkbook and disburse checks and make deposits based on your requests. You do not need to do this for closing a simple estate. As long as you feel you can keep and maintain accurate records and don't have a problem with organization, you should keep the checkbook and perform the disbursement of funds. It just gets cumbersome and expensive for the lawyer to keep the account. You'll need to present bills, request a check, track it and make the actual payment. Again, keeping accurate records is key but it's easily done.

Most of the monies you may pay out for the estate are for the upkeep of the house (while it is on the market) and for medical bills. There will be other bills that need to be paid out also. If you decide to have your lawyer keep the checkbook and disburse funds, make the request to the lawyer on a batch basis versus one at a time. For example, accumulate bills such as utilities, phone, insurance, and credit cards, and send them to the lawyer all at once to be paid versus sending them as they come in. It will be more efficient and cost less in the long run. One caveat: make sure that you don't miss a deadline by holding the bills past their due dates. As noted, it may be much easier and less costly to open the estate banking account and write checks yourself. Note that when you sign a check, you should write "Executor" under your name. That goes for any correspondence

Credit Cards: Start canceling the credit cards as soon as you can. There is no value in allowing credit card debt to pile up and also no need to expose the estate to any further liability from the unauthorized use of the credit cards. Call the credit card companies and verbally request cancellation of the credit account. Follow up with a letter stating the date and time of your phone conversation canceling the card and the name of the person with whom you spoke. Include in that letter copies of the letters testamentary and death certificate. Most major credit card companies will require simple copies as being acceptable; neither copy needs to be certified.

Mail: Forward the mail from the home of the deceased to yours, especially if the house will be vacant. You can simply fill out a change-of-address form on the United States Postal Service website[9] or locate the form in any post office to accomplish that. Complete the online Change of Address form, there will be a nominal fee. It is important to note that

---

[9] www.usps.com

mail forwarding based on the change-of-address form will expire one year from the date the form was filed. You must inform any creditors (e.g., the utility companies) that they must update their records to reflect the new address prior to the expiration of the Postal Service change-of-address.

Taxes: Your loved one will also most likely owe income tax (individual federal and state), and the estate may owe taxes (individual federal estate) based on its overall value. You should make sure that a separate file is maintained for all tax-related items (i.e., 1099 forms, statement of dividends, etc.) for the purposes of filing taxes with the state and federal governments. Do not overlook the filing of taxes for the estate. There are deadlines that must

Money will also continue to flow into and out of the estate, some of which will be taxable or tax deductible. You should also maintain a file for those items, which may affect the estate taxes owed. Some of those items are obvious, such as interest paid on the estate bank account, and clothing donations to a charity or expenses incurred from estate administration. Keep meticulous records, such as a diary with dates, names, places, and so on, which can be used if the Internal Revenue Service happens to audit either individual or estate returns.

You should file a change-of-address form with the IRS to ensure that all tax correspondence goes to you and to eliminate the possibility of the post office forwarding order expiring. The Change of Address is IRS form number 8822 (OMB #1545-1163) and can be obtained from the IRS website. Go to www.irs.gov and click on "Forms and Publications."

Generally you will need to file taxes at the end of the calendar year, but you may have to file quarterly taxes based on the person's income. Your lawyer can help provide practical and legal advice for this matter, or if you feel comfortable doing that work, you can do it yourself.

Chapter 12

Banking and IRAs

We've already read that the first thing you need to do is get organized. When you are working on the bank accounts, IRAs, CDs, and other banking information, first create manila folders so that statements can be sorted into the various groups and subgroups. For example, create banking folders organized by bank name. Then group items within that bank, such as certificates of deposit, checking accounts, and savings accounts. Determine how much money was in each based on the latest statement. Call each of the banks and let them know you'll be administering the estate. They will most likely not give you information about the account over the phone. They will, however, inform you of the process that they use in closing the account. They will go through the paperwork you will be expected to bring, including how signatures will be guaranteed (regular notary public or Medallion Guaranteed—see the securities section for definitions).

Safety Deposit Boxes. You need to check at each of the banks for a safety deposit box. Generally you can have the bank check by Social Security Number. Check even if you don't find a receipt or a key. It takes a minimal amount of time for the bank to determine if there is a safety deposit box in the decedent's name. Open the safety deposit box and make a record of the contents. You should do this early in your data-gathering phase. There may be important documents in the box. You do not need to remove the contents of the box; however, keep in mind that items must be distributed to the beneficiaries if they belonged to the decedent at the time he or she died. If an item was not owned by the deceased, it must be returned to the rightful owner as soon as is reasonable. There must be clear and irrefutable evidence that the property belonged to someone else before it is given to them. You don't want to take something out of the safety deposit box and give it to someone, only to find out it didn't belong to them and have to get it back.

You may be a co-owner of the safety deposit box with the decedent. For example, a mother and daughter own a safety deposit box together. When the mother passes away, the box and contents may or may not belong solely to the daughter. When opening a box that is jointly owned with no right of survivorship, the bank will generally have you sign paperwork that effectively says that, under penalty of perjury, all owners of the box are living. Please, please do not be tempted to falsely sign that statement if the other owner is deceased. The risk to your reputation, the loss of respect and trust, and/or the possibility of a fine or jail time are not worth any benefit you can get from signing that statement falsely.

Checking Accounts: The assumption that you can sign checks in the decedent's name from the decedent's checking account is false. Don't be tempted to write checks and sign them from the person's checking account because "it's easier" or something "has to be done right away." If you do, you are again jeopardizing the position of trust you are in. The beneficiaries may assume that since you have the checkbook and receive the bank statements that you can write checks to yourself, friends, shadow businesses, or any other entity of your choice. This is another situation where your actions must be beyond reproach. Close the checking account; destroy any ATM cards, save any and all statements for your records, and discuss this at your initial attorney review meeting.

To close a checking account you will need the following information:

- Decedent's Social Security Number
- Account number
- Amount from last statement (for your own verification)
- Affidavit of domicile, notarized
- Tax waiver form[10] (L-8 in New Jersey)
- Letters testamentary – original
- Certified copy of the death certificate
- Forms required by that particular bank

We recommend that you call the bank and set up an appointment with one of the bank officers to come in to close the account. They will be able to inform you of the paperwork required for closing the account and of any specific processes and procedures unique to that bank. The bank will generally close the account and hand you a certified check made out to the estate (i.e., Payable to the Estate of <decedent's name>).

---

[10]Currently only eight states require a tax waiver form.

You will then deposit the check in the estate account you have opened or mail it to the lawyer so he or she can make the deposit into the estate account. When endorsing checks, you should follow your signature with "Executor" and "For Deposit Only in Estate Account of <decedent's name>." By doing this, you ensure that should the check be stolen and subsequently cashed, the bank will be liable for not depositing the check into the estate account, not you.

Savings Accounts

The same information for closing a checking account is required for closing a simple savings account. You will need the following information:

- Decedent's Social Security Number
- Account number
- Amount from last statement (for your own verification)
- Affidavit of domicile, notarized
- Tax waiver form[11] (l-8 in New Jersey), notarized
- Letters testamentary—original
- Certified copy of death certificate
- Tax identification number
- Forms required by that particular bank

[11]Currently only eight states require a tax waiver form.

If the checking and savings accounts are in the same bank, they may not require duplicate affidavits of domicile, death certificates, and letters testamentary. It would be wise to check with the bank official while you are setting up the appointment to determine if you need the certified copies of forms for each of the accounts. As with checking accounts, a certified check will be issued payable to the estate. It should be endorsed as noted above, with "executor" and "for deposit only . . ." after your signature.

Certificates of Deposit

Certificates of Deposit (CD) require the same information (as checking and savings accounts) to close. As with the prior two types of accounts, the bank may not require duplicate certified copies of forms. Check with the bank officer to determine their requirements. There is a slight difference in closing certificates of deposit that you should be aware of. Typically there are maturity dates for CDs. For example a six-month CD opened in January will mature in June. At that time the money can be withdrawn and the interest applied in a normal situation. For an estate, usually the money can be withdrawn at any time without penalty. As with the other two types of bank accounts, a certified check payable to the estate will be issued. Unlike a checking or savings account, you may want to continue to keep the CD as it is. The basis for the decision is the amount of interest the CD is earning. If there is a high rate of interest for that particular CD and interest rates have fallen since its opening, you may want to keep the CD as is until the estate is closed.

Individual Retirement Accounts (IRAs)

Distribution of funds from an IRA does tend to be more complex than checking, savings, or certificates of deposit. The distribution schedule is made based on the age of the decedent and whether or not they had reached the mandatory age of distribution (70½). IRAs come in different flavors—i.e., Roth IRAs and traditional IRAs—and each have their own unique benefits for distribution. Beneficiaries of the IRA also have choices about how they want the funds distributed, for example, assuming the IRA, rolling the IRA over into another IRA, or moving the IRA to another financial institution. IRAs are also subject to applicable taxes.

It is important to note that IRAs are not part of the estate. You may hear the phrase that the IRA "passes outside the estate." This means the beneficiaries mentioned are the ones specified for the IRA itself, not the ones identified in the will. Why is this important to the executor? Even though "no good deed goes unpunished," the executor should provide a copy of the final IRA statement to the beneficiaries of record for the IRA so they are aware of the IRA value and that the IRA is designated directly to them, outside the estate. The beneficiaries can then contact the financial institution that holds the IRA and provide them with a certified copy of the death certificate. That institution will distribute the funds to the person named as a beneficiary for the IRA. The institution can also provide a copy of the rules for disbursing the IRA, with and without penalty. As noted, disbursement of funds from an IRA is not part of an executor duty, and the executor should take no action.

Trusts

Trusts are similar to IRAs in that there are different types: revocable, irrevocable, and living, among others. The other similarity is that trusts also pass outside the estate. If the deceased set up a trust, the person named as the trustee will make distributions to beneficiaries named in the trust documents. The executor has no duties and may only be asked to provide the trustee a copy of the death certificate.

Chapter 13

Securities

Selling or transferring securities is much easier than one would think and certainly does not require the services of an attorney. It also does not require having or opening a brokerage account. The key to being successful in the sale or transfer of stock is to know what paperwork is required to affect the sale/transfer and also to know the conditions under which the stock is held.

Before getting into how the stock sale and transfer works, it is worthwhile to define the various terms.

Transfer Agent: The transfer agent can be simply viewed as an entity similar to a bank savings account. It is not a person. The transfer agent is a company that holds the stock (like the bank holds your money); they prepare monthly or quarterly statements detailing how many shares you have, dividends reinvested or distributed, and other relevant information. They can sell stock (withdrawals) or they can buy stock for you (deposits). Appendix D has a list of transfer agents. They are companies whose names are likely to be familiar to you, such as Bank of New York Mellon, Computershare, and others. Visit the website of the company who issued the stock. You can usually find the name and contact information of the transfer agent under "Investor Relations - Stockholder Services." You can also search under "transfer agent". In addition, the latest stock statement will come from the transfer agent, so you can find their name and website there. An excellent resource is the Securities Transfer Association, www.stai.org as well in determining who the registered transfer agent is for those shares.

Stock Certificate: This is the physical certificate of stock. A stock will have the company name, number of shares, and certificate number printed on the face. Common stocks come in two forms: stock certificates and book entry shares. Very few shares are held in a physical form today, most are held electronically for ease of sale, etc…

Book Entry Shares: This simply refers to the number of stock shares held by the transfer agent. They in essence have the physical certificate for you in safekeeping and send you a statement listing your number of shares. You can always request a physical stock certificate from the transfer agent.

Direct Registration System (DRS): This is a service within the securities industry that allows shares to be held without a physical certificate. Not every transfer agent is signed up with the DRS.

Depository Trust Company Number (DTC #): This is similar to a routing number for a bank. It is a unique identifier for a transfer agent or other firm so that electronic routing of securities can be accomplished. You will need this number for your letter of instruction when transferring securities to each beneficiary's brokerage accounts (if you so choose). For the purposes of securities transfers, you can think of the DTC as one large vault with stock certificates in it. When you send a transfer request, they find the certificate, change the name on it, and reissue it per your instruction. You can call the particular brokerage house for their DTC number.

Medallion Signature Guarantee: "A statement (stamp and signature) given by a financial institution such as a commercial bank, credit union, brokerage firm, which are members of the Securities Transfer Association Medallion Program (STAMP), NY Stock Exchange Program or Stock Exchange Medallion Program (SEMP, MSP.) The Medallion Program ***is not a notarization.***"[12] One of the managers in your local bank branch will most likely be authorized to Medallion Guarantee your signature. All you will be required to provide are two forms of government identification, for example, a driver's license (with photo) or passport and a Social Security card.

Power of Attorney (POA): This document allows one person to act for another, limited by the instruction in the form. There are many types of power of attorney; some examples are to allow someone to sign your checks for you when you are medically unable or to enable a real estate transaction if you are not there. The power of attorney in a stock transfer or sale allows the transfer agent or brokerage firm to sell the stock on the open market for your benefit. That is the limit of what the firm can do with the power of attorney; they can't do anything else. In order to sell stock, you will need to complete this limited power of attorney form for the transfer agent.

Stocks are generally held in one of three ways: by a transfer agent (commonly known as the TA), a physical certificate (held by a private person), or by a brokerage firm, such as TD

[12]Securities Transfer Association

Ameritrade. Specific forms are required from transfer agents and brokerage firms to transfer or sell stock via the executor of an estate. Again, it is a simple, commonsense process once you understand how it works and what they want. In plain terms, the securities firm wants to know the following from you before they sell stock:

What They Want	*How to Answer*
How to Distribute Stocks	Letter of Instruction
Your authorization to sell or transfer stock	Stock Power Form
Proof you are authorized to act	Letters Testamentary
Proof no creditor will come back at a later time to claim stock	Order to Limit Creditors

Sample letters and forms are in the appendices, and a list with a short description follows:

- *Letter of Instruction:* This is a letter you create telling the transfer agent or brokerage what you want done with the securities. It should be the cover letter for all other forms. It should have the Social Security Number of the stock owner and the person to whom you want the stock transferred.

- *The Stock Power Form:* This form may look complicated and imposing, but it's really not. All you are doing is saying that the transfer agent is authorized to take the stock and distribute it according to your instructions. The signature on the form must be witnessed and stamped by a Medallion guarantor (commonly known as a Medallion Guarantee; see above). Most banks and securities firms will provide this service free of charge. The original stock power form must be submitted. A copy is not acceptable.

- *Affidavit of Domicile:* This form simply lets the firm know who the executor(s) is/are, where the decedent resided when they died, that debts are provided for, and that the distribution is according to the will. It is required because you as the executor are stating that everything is in order and the securities firm is not responsible for any liabilities of the estate. The signature on the form must be witnessed and stamped by a notary public. The original must be submitted. A copy is not acceptable.

- *Letters Testamentary:* This is the letter you receive from the surrogate judge saying you are the executor or co-executor of the estate. A certified copy (raised seal or stamp) must be submitted; a noncertified copy is not acceptable. It is important to note that you can go directly, without a lawyer, to the surrogate judge and receive, for a nominal fee, as many certified copies of the letters testamentary as you would like. For stock transfers, the letters testamentary must be dated within sixty days of the request. In other words, if the transfer agent receives the paperwork today, the letters testamentary cannot be dated more than sixty days ago. For clarity, if the transfer agent receives the paperwork on June 30, 2020, the letters testamentary can't be dated before April 30, 2020—it cannot be more than sixty days old. You should be prepared to request at least double the amount you think you'll need from the surrogate court. Many creditors, financial institutions, securities firms, etc… will need the Letters in order to execute your instructions. It just saves times from going back and forth with the surrogate court by obtaining more than you'll think you'll need.

- *Tax Waiver:* This form is required in fifteen states,[13] and it must signify who the beneficiaries are and what type (class) they are. For example, in New Jersey, if the beneficiaries are Class A (children of the deceased), there is no tax on the transfer. The signature on the form must be witnessed and stamped by a notary public. The original must be submitted. A copy is not acceptable.

- *Death Certificate:* You will need a certified copy (with raised seal) of the death certificate. One can be obtained from the board of health in the community (usually at the county level) in which the person died. They are available at a nominal fee, and you may need to provide the reason a death certificate is required. Many counties allow the request to be filed online. You do not need to go through the funeral home or the lawyer to obtain a copy. This is another opportunity for savings. It is suggested to obtain twice as many copies as you think you might need so that you don't need to go back multiple times to the BOH or administering entity, as a rule of thumb 20 copies might be a good number.

- *W-9:* This form may be required by some agents and not required by others. If it is required, use the decedent's name and tax identification number you previously obtained.

---

[13] AL, AZ, CT, IN, IA, LA, MT, NH, NJ, NY, NC, OK, OH, SD, TN. State requirements differ, so check with the tax department in the appropriate state.

It is advisable to send the forms to the transfer agent via certified mail, return receipt requested. If you are mailing the physical stock certificates to the agent for sale, send the forms and stock certificates registered mail and insure the mail for 2 percent of the total value of the securities. This would cover the cost of reissuing the certificate(s) to the estate in the event the certificate(s) is/are lost in the mail. You determine the insured value with the following formula:

Number of shares × current market price × 2% (.02) = insurance coverage

You may decide to forgo insurance because of the low value of the shares. For example, 100 certificated shares valued at $15.50 per share would have an insured value of $31 (100 × $15.50 = $1,550 × .02 = $31), not really worth the cost of the insurance. It's a decision you will have to make as the executor.

Of course, make copies of all the paperwork you send, the physical stock certificates and file it and the certified postal receipts in your newly developed and highly organized filing system along with the general estate paperwork. Also keep a record of the "basis date" for the stock. The basis date is the date when the stock passed to the estate. For example, if the person died on Thursday, July 14, 2020, the basis date is close of business on that day. The basis date is important because it will be used to calculate tax.

> For example, assume that on the date the person died he or she owned 1,000 shares of AT&T stock with each share valued at $12. On that day, the stock passes to

the estate with a basis (value) of $12 per share, $12,000 in total (1,000 shares × $12 per share = $12,000). The estate now owns stock valued at $12,000 as of that date. Assume the stock is sold three months later and each share is now worth $15. The gain for the estate would be the difference between $12 and $15 per share, $3,000 in total ($1,000 shares × $3 gain per). The $3,000 is taxable income for the estate because it's an actual monetary gain. It works the same way if the stock lost money; there would be an actual monetary loss and it would be reflected as such in the estate tax return.

The tax for the estate can be avoided with a transfer of the stock to each of the beneficiaries. With a transfer, there is no actual monetary gain or loss for the estate. The tax liability is transferred to beneficiaries, which allows them to sell or hold the stock based on their individual situations. Check with your certified public accountant for specific tax information.

You can expect a transfer to take place within one to two weeks of the transfer agent receiving the estate paperwork, assuming they have no questions and your paperwork is in order. Follow up with the individual transfer agents if you do not receive a confirmation of the transfer within three weeks or more. Typically, there is no fee charged for a stock transfer so long as another agent or brokerage will hold the stock. It is important to note that any fractional shares will be sold, and the proceeds distributed in a check to the transferee (beneficiary).

Once the transfer process has started, you may decide to get advice from your attorney about the proper forms the beneficiaries will sign upon receipt of the stock. It will most likely be as simple as their signature on a "partial refunding bond" indicating they received the stock and that if there is a problem, they will give it back.

One other option is to transfer the stock to an estate brokerage account. A brokerage will set up a special account for the estate, transfer the stock into the estate name, and hold, sell, or transfer the stock to the beneficiaries. Typically, there is a fee for these transactions by the brokerage. It may not be the best option because of the fees charged. You can consult your attorney for their advice about which option to choose. In most instances, the recommended course of action is to transfer the stock to the beneficiaries so they have the tax liability and can make their own individual decisions on whether to hold, sell, or partially sell the stock.

Lost Shares: The transfer agent can help with reissuing certificates that were lost or stolen. To have them reissued, you will sign an affidavit saying that they were in fact lost and outlining the circumstances behind the loss. Then you must purchase an indemnity bond to hold the corporation and the transfer agent harmless should the certificate be presented at a later date by an "innocent" purchaser. The indemnity bond usually costs about 3 percent of the fair market value of the security. Most transfer agents have the proper forms and instructions on their websites.

Chapter 14

Selling the House

Selling the house is probably the largest transaction you will affect during the course of closing the estate. It is also probably one of the more emotional transactions because it may be the place where the beneficiaries grew up, it's the last vestige of the deceased, and/or it is the last item that needs to be wrapped up before the estate is closed and people can move on.

You need to realize that selling real estate in normal circumstances is usually driven more by emotion than by logic. Couple that with selling real estate for your deceased loved one and you will find that emotion can cloud your judgment.

Keep the House or Sell It? Sell it! Sell it! Sell it! You may be tempted to keep it and rent it because it's a "down" real-estate market at the moment. Forget that strategy. Let's say you plan to keep it for a year while the market turns. At the end of the year the market is worse. Now you've got the beneficiaries complaining that the value of the house is lower, the time value based on the cash from a quick sale is less, and you've lost one year of carrying charges. Let's look at it the other way and say the market turns up over the year. Chances are that if you weigh all the factors, such as time value of money and carrying charges, you might break even or be slightly ahead.

You'll get no awards for that. Let's say the house burns down during that year. Do you think you'll be chastised for keeping the house or that the beneficiaries will tell you not to worry about it? You are most likely far better off getting market value for the house and getting it off your hands.

Selecting a Real-Estate Agent: Keep in mind that the largest fee that the estate will pay will probably be to the real-estate agent. The real-estate agent will also have a great influence over the amount you will market the home for and the price you finally settle on. Because of this, the selection of the agent is very important. As with the selection of a lawyer, the recommendation is to select a real-estate agent who is not part of the family, a family friend, or anyone you know. You should do this for a number of reasons. It takes any claim of conflict of interest away from the executor. It makes it easier to fire the agent if that particular situation arises, and it also ensures that there is no undercurrent of allegiance to any other family member or beneficiary while the deal is in process.

Before you contact any real-estate firms to begin the selection process, you should take some time to prepare. You should understand your goals, the questions you need to ask during the selection process, and how you will make your final decision.

As this must be an unemotional decision, we recommend that one of your goals be to sell the house as quickly as reasonably possible for fair market value. The recommendation stems from the estate paying the home's carrying costs each month it is not sold. It also carries risk (for example, as noted earlier, if the house burns down, it needs to be rebuilt) and the executor must expend time and energy regularly checking on the property. Insurance companies typically will not fully insure a vacant house. Having limited insurance is much too great a risk for the estate to carry. This is atypical of a situation where one sells their house to buy another. The carrying costs are not lost because the person/people in the house still receive the benefit of living there, the heat and light from paying the utility bills, the phone, and all other household expenses. The estate gets no benefit from the carrying costs; they are expenditures that aren't recovered and continue to mount over time. To illustrate this point, see the following chart, which compares a home being sold for the same $200,000 in January and in June (same year).

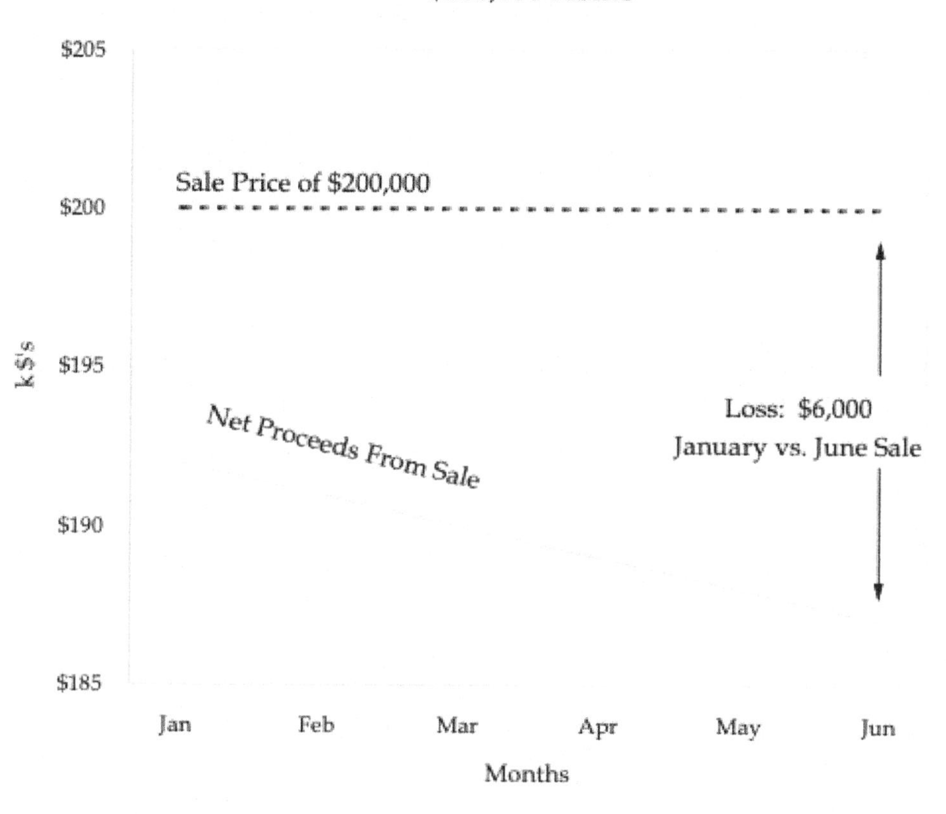
Sale in January vs. Sale in June
$200,000 Home
$205
Sale Price of $200,000
$200
k$'s
$195
Net Proceeds From Sale
Loss: $6,000
January vs. June Sale
$190
$185
Jan
Feb
Mar
Apr
May
Jun
Months

The chart on the previous page assumes a selling price of $200,000. If the house is sold in January, the net cash to the estate is about $192,000 (after all costs). If the house is sold in June for the same $200,000, the net cash the estate will receive is about $186,000, a difference of $6,000. The $6,000 is made up of the carrying costs and the time value of money. You need to be aware of this as you price the house with the real-estate agent, negotiate a sale price with the buyer, and determine the closing date.

Even if the real-estate market is rising, it is less risky and more responsible to sell the house and put the money into a safe, short-term, interest-bearing account, perhaps a bank certificate of deposit.

As with the selection of a lawyer, interview a minimum of three real-estate agents from three different firms. Some of the questions you should ask (and acceptable answers to expect) are listed below.

- *How long have you been a real-estate agent?* Typically, you would like to hire someone with at least five years of experience in selling homes. You want someone who understands the ins and outs of the listing service, knows how to deal with lawyers and other real-estate agents, and has some type of track record.

- *How many estate homes have you sold?* This is another question about the agent's level of experience. There are some nuances in selling an estate home versus your own. For example, the lawyer representing the home sale (a different transaction from estate representation) should suggest a clause stipulating that the results of the home inspection not be used to renegotiate the price of the home (estates are usually take-it-or-leave-it). The real-estate agent should be experienced enough to understand the reason for that clause and explain it to the buyer's agent.

- *How many homes of this type have you sold?* You are trying to determine the agent's experience and activity. An average of one or two homes per month (more than twelve annually) is acceptable.

- *What is the average sale price of homes you have sold?* You're simply trying to determine if this agent understands the needs of buyers in your particular selling range. If the listing price for the property is $200,000 and the agent's average sale price is $500,000, he or she may not be as aware of what drives a $200,000 buyer.

- *How many listings do you currently have?* This is another question designed to determine how active this agent is. Having a small number of listings (less than five or so) may indicate a lack of experience or expertise.

- *Will you be willing not to be a disclosed dual agent?* A disclosed dual agent is a real-estate agent who can represent both the buyer and the seller. Because of the nature of that relationship, they may not always act in your (the estate's) best interests. They will negotiate on behalf of both the buyer and seller. There is always the appearance of an inherent conflict whereby the estate pays the agent a sizable fee and yet the agent is not always representing the estate's best interests, because they cannot negotiate in favor of either party. In a dual-agent situation, the agent/broker is no longer your advocate. It is strongly recommended that the real-estate contract (listing agreement) specifically say that the broker and real-estate agent will not be dual agents and will act only as the seller's agent.

- *What is the average difference between asking and selling price in this area for this type of home?* Have the agent commit to a number that is based solely on facts and have him or her show you the listing and selling prices for those homes. This number will give you a general idea of what a reasonable offer is for the property and what you may be willing to accept. For example, if comparable houses in the area list for $200,000 and the final sale price is $190,000 (a 5 percent difference), you should be willing to entertain offers in that general range. More important, you should not waste your time with offers significantly below that floor.

- *What is the average difference between asking and selling prices for homes you have listed?* This is a test of the real-estate agent's ability to price a home for fair market value. Have the agent show you the homes he or she has listed over the past year and compare those listing and selling price averages against all homes in the area. If the agent is not within 1 percent, plus or minus, of the average for the area, find a new agent.

- *What are your thoughts on your being at the closing?* Many times, especially when the potential exists for a contentious closing, the real-estate agent will not attend. It is recommended that the agent, at a minimum, be available for the closing in the event that any last-minute issues occur. This is a decision that you and your real-estate lawyer will make before closing. If the agent will not commit to being at the closing, find a new agent. It is not always a bad thing, however, for the agent not to be at the closing. It could be a tactic to prevent last-minute changes from being made. It comes down to how comfortable you feel with the agent's answer to this question and his or her explanation.

- *What is your recommendation for the listing price?* When presenting the recommendation, the real-estate agent should include other comparable home sales in the area. The agent should also be able to articulate why your home should sell for more or less and faster or more slowly than is typical.

- *What can be done to enhance the home's "curb appeal"?* This is a question designed to subjectively test the agent's selling skills. If you feel that the home is in relatively good condition, and the agent has an inordinate number of suggestions about repairs, painting, wallpaper, and so on, you should be wary. You want to make only those repairs or investments that you can recoup either in a higher listing price or in a faster sale.

> For example, if the agent says that in their opinion, painting two rooms for a cost of $500 will result in raising the listing price by $2,000, painting those two rooms may be a good investment. If, on the other hand, the agent suggests painting those same two rooms and can't articulate the return in value, he or she may not be experienced enough in real-estate sales.

You should also check to see if there are any complaints filed against the real-estate agent you are in the process of selecting. In New Jersey you can go to the website www.state.nj.us/dobi/remnu.htm, which is the home page of the New Jersey Real Estate Commission (part of the Department of New Jersey Banking and Insurance) and check an agent's status by name. You can also view any complaints lodged against that particular agent. Other states have similar online sites to check real-estate agents. It pays to do due diligence.

Insurance Considerations: First and foremost, make sure that the homeowners' insurance does not lapse. At the same time, make sure that there is enough coverage on the house and furnishings (if it is to remain furnished for any period of time). This is another area where the estate is potentially exposed to a great risk. It's fairly obvious that if you let the insurance coverage lapse and the house burns to the ground, you have lost a significant portion of the value of the estate. The same holds true if the house is undervalued for insurance purposes. If the house is insured for $100,000, is worth $250,000, and burns down, you will recover only $100,000 (less the deductible), again resulting in a significant loss for the estate. You must also consider furnishings in the house, making sure they are insured for replacement value. Categorize furnishings/belongings and photograph and/or video all the rooms in the house including appliances, pots/pans, anything in drawers/cabinets - all the nooks and crannies in the house. This serves a number of purposes. If the house burns down or is damaged in some way, you have a record of what was in the house when you file a claim. It also documents the majority of the furnishings/belongings, which will be distributed among the beneficiaries. Another insurance item is that of a vacant-house policy. The insurance company may want to insure the house as a vacant house. Vacant-house policies typically insure only for fire. This means that the house is not insured if there is a water leak or a tree falls on the house. Try to negotiate around this by letting them know the house is on the market or that you inspect the house every day (if either are the case, of course) because, as always, you want to mitigate the risk to the estate as much as possible. One final item is to request a prorated refund for the balance of the homeowners' insurance premium once the house is sold. A sample letter is attached in Appendix E.

Other Considerations and Recommendations

• *Don't rent the house*: Unless the property is already rented or is in a neighborhood that has other rental properties, don't rent the house. It may affect your ability to sell it, it may cause your insurance rate to increase, and it may increase the risk to the estate because of additional liability issues. Another issue is that the renter may not want to leave once the house is sold, even if they have a month-to-month lease. If this happens, you will need to file with the local court to evict the tenant and go through that process, which could take months at a minimum.

• *Don't allow beneficiaries to take up residence:* Again, unless the beneficiaries currently live in the house, don't expose the estate to unnecessary or greater risk. Although living in the house may protect against vandalism and other "vacant-home" risks, you may not be able to sell as quickly if the occupants are encumbered with finding another residence. It also may result in issues between beneficiaries because of the real or perceived benefit to one versus another.

• *Let the real-estate agent show the house:* Don't be there when the agent is showing the house to a prospective buyer. Allow the agent to do his or her job unencumbered. Also, allow the agent to install a lock box so that prospective buyers can tour the house at their convenience. It increases the potential for a quicker sale too.

- *Keep furniture in the house:* Don't take the furniture out of the house; have it look as if someone continues to live there. It's cold and impersonal to look at empty rooms. Try, however, to remove all the clutter and "stage" the house, using the theory that less is more. You may be comfortable with having the dining table, hutch, sideboard, easy chairs, and tea cart in the dining room, but all that furniture makes the room look much smaller than it is. Keep ample walkways. Remove most of the personal photos, declutter the electronics, minimize the number of "products" in the bathroom, and just generally make it look like a model home. Go to the Internet and get ideas from professional home stagers along with following your real-estate agent's advice.

- *Keep the attractive selling points in mind:* You have a number of advantages if the home is vacant. You should be able to offer a quick closing, which enables the buyer to move in quickly. You do not need to make the sale of the home contingent on the purchase of another home, so there is less of a chance that the deal will fall through. The house will also show better: it will always be clean, there won't be any offensive cooking odors, and the prospective buyers will be able to look through every room, every closet, and in bathrooms and cabinets without the fear of disturbing anything or anybody.

You may have the situation where one or more of the beneficiaries wants to purchase the house. If only one wants to buy the house, retain a real-estate appraiser, not an agent, to assess the fair market value of the property. The estate can then sell the house to that beneficiary. The proceeds will be deposited into the estate account and become part of the distribution when the final accounting for the estate is complete. If more than one beneficiary wants to purchase the house, they will need to negotiate between or among themselves and come to an agreement on which one will get the house. If they cannot reach agreement, put the house on the market and sell it via a real-estate agent.

One strong recommendation in these circumstances is to be sure you sell the house at fair market value. You cannot allow or have the appearance of allowing one beneficiary to have financial advantage by receiving a "discount" for the house.

Chapter 15

Distributing a Coin Collection

This is another "can't win so don't try" area. The coin collection may be another one of those sentimental items that causes great acrimony over something that will probably have relatively little value. Another acrimonious dynamic is the assumption that the coin collection will be a source of great wealth. This is usually not the case. Ninety-eight percent of old coins (pre-1964)—even those from the nineteenth century—are not worth much more than ten times their face value and usually are worth much less. This means that a coin collection with approximately 700 coins would be worth about $1,200 retail. This would represent 2/10 of 1 percent (.2%) of a $500,000 estate, retail. As you can see, there is no need to squabble over such a low percentage sum, but, because there is sentimental value attached and/or the beneficiaries may think one rare coin worth hundreds of thousands of dollars is involved, there is room for great argument.

To avoid such an end, there are two recommendations for administering a coin collection:

- *Sell it:* Take the collection and get an appraisal from three reputable coin traders. It is key that you do your due diligence for coin traders, because you will most likely have to rely on their expertise for the value of the coin collection. Also note that they will quote you the price they are willing to pay for the coins so that they can resell them. The downside is that they may offer 50–75 percent below the retail value, so in the example above, those coins may fetch only $600. You should also determine value by looking at some of the coin auction sites (check via the Internet) and also on eBay It is also important to determine if the collection has more value intact versus selling each coin on an individual basis.

◆ *Distribute it:* Divide the physical coins as equally as possible. This is not an exact science because of the somewhat subjective nature of the value and grading of the coins. If you think there is any possibility that one or some of the coins has great worth, have an appraisal done.

A methodology that can be used to do a distribution is as follows:

◆ Sort all the coins into their various denominations.

◆ Sort the denominated coins by year.

◆ Determine if any of the coins has a material relative value over any of the other coins.[14] Put those coins off to the side.

◆ Take the remaining coins and distribute them equally among the number of beneficiaries by denomination. For example, if there are twelve 1964 quarters and three beneficiaries, each person gets four 1964 quarters. That way the split is even.

◆ If the coins can't be divided among the beneficiaries evenly by year, go to the next year in sequence. For example, if there

[14] You can make that determination by reviewing an up-to-date coin-pricing book. One such book is *2012 North American Coins & Prices,* by Krause Publications, 2012.

are ten 1964 quarters and two 1963 quarters and three beneficiaries, each beneficiary will still get four quarters; however, two of them will get 1963 coins. Just keep moving on down the line that way.

Figure 1: Coin Distribution

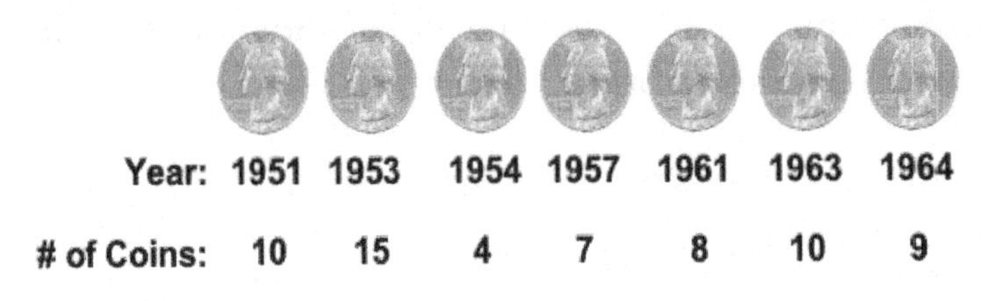

In the figure above, assume there are three beneficiaries. Start from the right and work to the left. For 1964, each beneficiary would receive three coins (9 / 3 = 3). For 1963 coins, each again would receive three, with one left over (10 / 3 = 3 with 1 left). Add the one left-over 1963 coin to the 1961 pile (making nine coins) and then divide them again and so on down the line. As stated above, if the coins are assumed to be of relative equal value, this is a reasonable way to make the distribution without having to sell them.

By doing this, you also avoid the situation where one of the beneficiaries thinks the coins should be sold, whereas the others do not. If you divide them equally based on the relative value, that one beneficiary can sell his or her share of the coins and the others can retain them.

Another choice would be to put the coins in a pile and ask each beneficiary to select a coin in turn until they are all gone. This is a simple and fair way to distribute them if other accommodations cannot be agreed to.

In summary, keep in mind that no good deed goes unpunished; therefore, the recommendation is to review this strategy with the lawyer, divide the coins equally as quickly as possible, and be done with it.

Chapter 16

Distributing Jewelry

This is another one of those areas that deserves a chapter of its own because of the potential for a high amount of acrimony versus the unemotional real value of the property. Jewelry is probably the most sentimental of personal belongings that a one can have. A piece of jewelry is usually given to someone for a special occasion versus purchased by and for oneself, which makes the item hold even more sentimental value. Once you take a cold and unemotional viewpoint, you will probably find that the jewelry is not worth as much as you think.

You'll most probably run into one or more of the beneficiaries having given jewelry as a gift to the deceased and therefore expecting to have that jewelry distributed back to them. Daughters who are beneficiaries may expect to receive their mother's rings, necklaces, bracelets, and the like because of the fact that they are traditionally women's items. This is especially true for engagement rings and wedding bands: they "belong" to the daughter(s). They may even believe that the rings are theirs inherently and not part of the estate. This is not the case (unless the will specifically states the contrary). All the jewelry, if it is not discreetly spelled out in the will, belongs to the estate and must be distributed reasonably, equitably, and fairly. To make sure there are no misconceptions, make sure that you review the distribution of property, especially jewelry, with the beneficiaries in your initial meeting with the lawyer.

The first thing you should do when planning for the distribution of jewelry is to find out what it's worth. As with a coin collection, there are typically two ways of distributing jewelry. You can sell it and distribute the cash or you can make the physical distribution among the beneficiaries.

- *Sell it:* If you decide to sell the jewelry, you will first need to get estimates on its value, both as a collection and as individual pieces. There are a number of methods to determine value. The most obvious is to take the jewelry to a store and ask them to appraise each of the pieces and give you a price. You can find jewelry auctions in newspapers and on the Internet, and you can also do the auction yourself via eBay You can also use a classified advertisement in the newspaper (although this is not recommended because you don't know who you will be dealing with). If you decide to sell the jewelry to a retailer, it's important to realize that you will probably receive half of the wholesale price for the piece of jewelry. That means that if the piece retails for $2,000 and wholesales for $1,000, you will receive half of the wholesale, or $500. See Appendix C for a number of resources you can use to educate yourself about the various methods of selling estate jewelry. Also be aware that most jewelry will not sell as jewelry but for the value of the precious metal (e.g., gold) and/or stone (e.g., diamonds) it contains. There just isn't that much of a market for individual pieces. What the jeweler will most likely do is melt the gold and sell the diamonds to make new pieces. If you can avoid it, don't take your pieces to a pawnshop. Pawnshops typically offer you 40 to 50 percent of the value of the item.

- *Distribute it:* This is not an easy task either. There will be various pieces of jewelry with very disparate values. There will be arguments about who gets which piece and who is more deserving of a particular piece. For example, the estate has one diamond solitaire engagement ring valued at about $7,000, one diamond wedding band valued at $3,000, and three beneficiaries, two daughters and a son. Both daughters want the engagement ring and wedding band. The son wants neither. Distributing two rings among the three beneficiaries won't be equitable, so there needs to be a method by which the jewelry can become part of a larger "pie." This may include cash from the overall estate settlement or out of pocket from a beneficiary. If jewelry is to be distributed, it is better to place it into the entire group of property so tradeoffs can be made.

Although it is certainly a reasonable course of action to sell the jewelry, it is not recommended for a number of reasons. The beneficiaries may want some or all of the pieces. If you sell the pieces and tell the beneficiary to buy it from the retailer if they want it, they may experience a 300 percent markup. That is inherently unfair when a distribution could be made. If, on the other hand, the beneficiaries want the cash for the jewelry, they can receive the distribution and then sell it on their own. This avoids a number of issues. First, it eliminates the time and expense to get the appraisals and/or the agreements with an auction house or retailer/wholesaler. It removes any inkling of the executor not getting a fair sale price. It also preserves the long-term value of the jewelry for the beneficiary.

Jewelry distribution is another part of the estate that is not as easily quantifiable as cash, securities, or even real estate. By taking an approach where the beneficiaries decide on a fair and equitable distribution that is "envy-free," you won't be the one who made the "wrong" decision. If you sell the jewelry, you may be accused of not getting a fair price for it. If you distribute the jewelry, you will be accused of doing it inequitably. Do what is reasonable, fair, and equitable; attempt to have the beneficiaries determine what a fair distribution is, document everything, and you will be much happier for it.

Chapter 17

Dividing Other Property

There is yet another area where problems can arise because of the sentimental nature of heirlooms or property of the deceased. There may be antique furniture passed down through generations or perhaps a fur coat given as a silver-anniversary present. Even an old photograph of a grandparent can elicit some level of greed or envy. One person may find the intrinsic value of such items far greater or less than another. The actual cash value of furniture and other possessions is very difficult and time consuming to ascertain. When other property of the estate is divided, one (or more) of the beneficiaries may feel that another received "more" than a fair share. This is because of the inexact and subjective nature of the valuation of possessions versus cash and cash equivalents (i.e.. stocks, bonds, CDs, and so on). Cash does not have an envy factor associated with it because its division is totally objective. There should not be a rational feeling of unfair division. If there is $100 cash and there are two beneficiaries, each receives $50; neither can rationally argue that the other received more or less than a fair share.

The fair division of items in an estate does not mean the equal division of items. This is simply because you can't equally divide certain items, such as an original portrait of a parent. Also, one beneficiary may place a higher value on a particular item than another beneficiary, so the true value for these items is very difficult (if not impossible) to determine. There are probably some items that have no monetary value at all but have a high value placed on them by one (or more) beneficiary. The portrait of a parent may have no fair market value; however, it is priceless and irreplaceable to a beneficiary.

One method by which to fairly divide the possessions is discrete mathematics, sometimes called "fair mathematics." It is far less formidable than it sounds, and if you use the spreadsheet on our website (www.executorbook.com - click on the 'templates' tab), it should be simple to do. It allows items that obviously cannot be *equally divided* by splitting (such as the portrait in the example above or the family dog) to be *fairly divided* between or among a group of beneficiaries. The concept of fair math considers that there are a number of items within the estate that must be fairly divided among beneficiaries. It assumes that the items can't be sold without them losing much of their value, that they may actually have no fair market value (e.g., the portrait or the dog) but are wanted items, and that the items cannot be physically divided, like the dog. Fair math also mitigates the envy factor because each of the beneficiaries receives what they consider to be a fair share, no more and no less.

Implementing a fair math distribution of the items is a four-step process:

1. List each of the items in the estate that will be part of the fair math division. Provide that list to each of the beneficiaries. Review the list with them and remove or add items to the list as appropriate. For example, based on input from the beneficiaries, items such as coffeepots or kitchen utensils may or may not be on the list. It all depends on the level of detail

and the amount of time all beneficiaries are willing to agree to when ascertaining value.

2. Once the list is final, have each beneficiary place the monetary value or "bid" they think the item is worth next to each item on the list. To eliminate any collusion, the bid must be sealed and not shared with any other beneficiary. If the beneficiary wants the item, they will place a high bid on it; if not, they will place a low bid on it, just as in an auction.

3. Determine which beneficiary receives the item based on the highest bid.

4. Total the highest bids for each beneficiary. Then divide that total by the number of beneficiaries. This becomes the amount owed or paid by each beneficiary for the fair value of those items.

It is a bit complicated, but the examples below illustrate how it's done and how the envy factor is eliminated. We'll assume only one item in this example—the portrait. Figure 1 below lists the bids from each of the beneficiaries for the portrait:

Figure 2: Fair Math Example—One Item (Portrait)

BENEFICIARY				
Item	**John**	**Daniel**	**Barbara**	**Winning Bid**
Portrait	$2,500	$3,500	$3,000	Daniel-$3,500
			TOTAL:	**$3,500**

In Figure 1, each of the beneficiaries uses a sealed bid for the portrait, bidding what the portrait is worth to them. Daniel submits the winning bid of $3,500, his view of its worth. Because he views the portrait as being worth $3,500, he should expect to compensate each of the beneficiaries $1,167 ($3,500 ÷ 3 = $1,167), their share of the portrait. John and Barbara have no other choice than to agree that it's fair (free from envy) because they thought the value of the portrait was less, yet they are being compensated more. Had either of their bids been the highest one, they would have had to compensate the other beneficiaries, $833 (John) or $1,000 (Barbara). They are getting more cash than they would have had to give.

The portrait in the above example could be replaced by any possession that would require a King Solomon-type of resolution (splitting the baby in half). Examples would be a family Bible, a childhood toy, an original manuscript—anything that cannot be divided. One may consider the alternative of sharing the possession. For example, in year one, the portrait hangs in John's house, in year two it hangs in Daniel's, in year three it hangs in Barbara's, and in year four it goes back to John. This method is not recommended, however, because it may cause ownership problems in the future among beneficiaries of the beneficiaries.

Another example for distributing multiple items follows in Figure 3:

Figure 3: Fair Math Example—Multiple Items

		BENEFICIARY		
ITEM	**John**	**Daniel**	**Barbara**	**Winning Bid**
Ring	$400	$900	$600	**$900**
Table	$400	$200	$500	**$500**
Couch	$400	$200	$300	**$400**
Book	$900	$800	$500	**$900**
			TOTAL:	**$2,700**

In the figure above, the total fair market value of the items as determined by the beneficiaries is $2,700. John had the winning bid for the couch and book, Daniel the winning bid for the ring, and Barbara the winning bid for the table. Each now has the benefit of the item for which he or she submitted the winning bid. However, they need to complete another step to ensure fairness.

To determine what is fair, we look at the sum of the winning bids ($2,700) as the fair value of the items without regard to who received what. The $2,700 being the fair value, each beneficiary is entitled to $900 ($2,700 ÷ 3 beneficiaries = $900). Use the chart in the figure below, which presents the total of winning bids by individual:

Figure 4: Total of Winning Bids

Beneficiary	Total of Winning Bids
John	$1,300
Daniel	$900
Barbara	$500
TOTAL	**$2,700**

John receives $1,300 worth of items (the couch and book), Daniel $900 (ring), and Barbara $500 (table). That being the case, John owes the estate $400 ($1,300 value less the $900 equal share = $400 owed), Daniel owes $0 ($900 in value less the $900 equal share), and Barbara is owed $400.

If one of the beneficiaries did not get any of the items, they must be made aware that they received more cash than the other beneficiaries and also that they received more than they thought each of the items was worth. Let's assume that we have two items, a clock and a chair, and the same three beneficiaries as above. See the figure below.

Figure 5: Two Items, Three Beneficiaries

ITEM	John	Daniel	Barbara	Winning Bid
Clock	$100	$200	$300	**$300**
Chair	$300	$200	$100	**$300**
				$600

In this example, there are only two items to be distributed among three people. Barbara would receive the clock, John would receive the chair, and Daniel, who received no property, would be compensated $200, one-third of the $600 total.

The envy factor comes into play when a beneficiary(s) believes the possessions in an estate were divided unfairly and inequitably. The envy factor can be illustrated in its simplest form by thinking of the "cake division" problem taught in discrete mathematics classes. Two children are given a cake to share. Assume that if one child cuts the cake and takes a piece, the other child may believe that he or she got a smaller piece of cake; hence, the second child envies the first child's larger piece. To avoid the envy issue, both children agree that the first child will cut the cake and the second child will select the first piece. In that way, the concern about inequitable distribution is significantly reduced.

It is time consuming to actually sell the other possessions either via an estate sale or to a liquidator, and again, the real value won't be realized. If the beneficiaries can agree upon a fair distribution, the executor can save time and also costs for the estate.

There are quite a number of methods for distributing the possessions. Keep in mind that they all are correct if the beneficiaries all agree that they are correct. If you refer to the jewelry example, the two rings valued at $7,000 and $3,000 were to be divided among three beneficiaries (two daughters and a son). If the beneficiaries all agree that the fair distribution of the rings is one ring to each daughter and none to the son, with no compensation for the son, it is still viewed as equitable *because all the beneficiaries agree.*

Chapter 18

Selling the Car

There are a number of avenues to take when selling the car, and there multiple reasonable courses of action. There is no one way that is better than another, a specific situation determines the specific course of action. There are a few consistencies for each of the scenarios when disposing of the car; the title must be signed by the executor(s) and a certified copy of the letters testamentary must be attached to the title.

It is very important when selling the car to:

- take the license plates or tags off the car (for return to the motor vehicle agency), and

- obtain a receipt from the motor vehicle agency for the plates/tags and go with the buyer to the motor vehicle agency to change the title.

These above steps are important because they limit the estate's liability if the car is involved in an accident. For example, you sell the car to Joe, sign over the title, and drop the car off to him on Wednesday. Joe takes the car out to dinner Thursday evening, has a few drinks, and is involved in a bad accident. The police see the motor vehicle records listing the car as belonging to the estate (decedent), not to Joe. Joe tears up the title and says you lent him the car for a test drive only. You wouldn't have anything to refute that claim (your word against Joe's), and you would probably end up in court defending the estate. Granted it's very unlikely that would happen, but it's worth the small investment of time to formally transfer ownership to avoid the risk of having a lawsuit against the estate.

The options you have in selling the car are generally as follows:

- Sell it yourself
- Wholesaling the car to an auctioneer
- Wholesaling the car to a dealer
- Paying a flat fee for a dealer to sell the car
- Donating the car to charity
- Distributing it as property to beneficiaries

The option you choose will depend on the amount of time you have to dispose of the car and the type of car it is (i.e., you may choose different options for a high-end luxury car than for a low-end, utilitarian, older car). You also need to consider the carrying costs for the car. You must continue to carry auto insurance until the car is sold, you may have to pay storage, and you'll have to start it at least once per week or preferably drive it at least that frequently. You need to weigh those factors against the options and make the decision relative to your particular situation. The options are discussed in more detail below:

1. *Wholesaling the car to an auctioneer:* This is attractive because you can have the car sold in one day. Typically, you drive the car to their lot; they give you cash for the car and a proof-of-purchase receipt (to eliminate your liability). The downside to this method is that you will get the lowest possible price for the car. For example, depending on the type of car, they may discount it up to 40 percent (which means they will pay you $6,000 for a car worth $10,000 retail). This is still a reasonable, fair, and equitable way to dispose of a car; therefore, depending on the circumstances, you may want to use this method. It is relatively painless, and you can get an estimate of what they will pay for the car over the phone or on the Internet. This will save a significant amount of time in disposing of the car. One additional benefit is that there is no implied warranty on the car. In other words, they won't be calling you if the car breaks down the next day, asking for their money back. Some of the resources you can use to wholesale a car are in Appendix C.

2. *Placing a classified advertisement:* Many people sell cars this way. Just look through your local Sunday paper, internet classifieds, E-bay, Craigslist, etc... and you will see countless cars for sale. This is where you will get the highest price for the car, because you will be asking for the retail price. This method has a number of downsides, however, some of them based on your individual perspective and some financial. People you do not know will be coming to your home. That may not be something you feel comfortable with, especially if you have young children. You won't know if the person is qualified to buy the car. They may not have the financial resources available, yet they may waste your time looking at the car and taking it for a test drive. You will have

to negotiate price, again, something that you might find uncomfortable. Regarding test drives, you will have the liability of another driver in the car. If they have an accident, you may pass that liability on to the estate. Test drives also go back to the "stranger" issue; you are now in a car with someone you don't know. It's another item you may or may not be comfortable with. Retailing the car is when you must take a firm position on the title transfer. When the person buys the car, make sure that you remove the license plates and go with him or her to the motor vehicle agency to transfer title. It is a hassle, and you may find it embarrassing to impose this requirement on the buyer, but if you don't do it, you expose the estate to great liability. You must insist on payment for the car with a certified check, bank check, or cash, because again, you will open the estate to liability if you relinquish title without receiving proper payment. One last thought is that you may run into a situation where the buyer wants to return the car. Generally a buyer has the right to return the car and receive a refund within three days of purchase. You may have to deal with that if you decide to sell the car through a classified ad. As with anything sold retail, it's not easy dealing with the public.

3. *Wholesaling a car to a dealer:* This works almost the same way as selling to an auctioneer; however, you will have to spend more of your time shopping the car with this method. You'll need to call dealers for that particular make of car, because dealers will not typically take other makes when buying (versus accepting a trade-in). For example, a Chrysler dealer won't be interested in buying a General Motors car. Auctioneers give you the money on the spot, no questions asked. Dealers will want to see the car and possibly take it for a test drive, and are more apt to turn you down (or give you a low price) if they don't think they can move the car quickly. The issue of liability also comes into question with a test drive; however, it is not as great as with a private sale through a classified. The liability issue of title transfer is not relevant here, because the dealer will give you a valid receipt/proof of purchase for the car on the spot.

4. *Donating the car:* You've all heard the television advertisements asking for donated vehicles. Many charitable organizations are using car donations as a way of generating contributions. This is a viable option and one worth consideration if the car has relatively low value. This is another area where you must do your research, because there are some groups for which the government will not allow a tax deduction. You also need to determine if they will pick up the car for free or for a fee. You will need to put your personal bias aside when making such a decision. You may feel it is altruistic to donate the car to a worthy cause; however, as with all other possessions of the estate, *the car belongs to the estate, not to you.* Giving a donation to a charitable organization solely because you feel compelled to give is not appropriate. See Appendix C for those organizations that will accept cars for donation. Consult your tax adviser about how the estate can benefit from a donation of the car. Also consult Internal Revenue Service Publication 526 (Charitable Contributions)[15] for background in determining if your car and/or charity is qualified so that the estate can receive an IRS deduction.

5. *Distribution as property:* This simply means including the car as part of the overall property—for example, furniture—distribution. Assign value to the car as you would

---

[15] www.irs.gov/pub/irs-pdf/p526.pdf

any other piece of property, and either have the beneficiary who wants it pay for it or take a lesser amount of other estate property to offset the value. This is not recommended because it adds to the "envy factor" where the other beneficiaries may think the beneficiary who gets the car gets a better deal than the others. The car should not have sentimental value (unless it is classified an antique or historic vehicle) and therefore should be sold via one of the methods suggested above.

As with selling anything, the most effective way to get the best price is to be armed with knowledge of the value of what you are selling. There are a number of excellent resources on the Internet that will give you both the retail and the wholesale value of the car. Kelley Blue Book is one good example of an Internet site where you can determine retail and wholesale pricing for a car for a particular geographic location. We recommend that you use all the resources available to determine the fair market value of the car so that you can negotiate from a position of strength or include it as part of the distribution of property for the estate.

Lease: If the car is leased, the estate generally has a continuing obligation for the remaining balance. There are a number of options as follows.

- Continue the payments: The estate can continue to pay the lease monthly and continue to use the car. This option isn't the best one because of the liability. Even if the car is insured, the estate is responsible for any payment or judgment against it in the event of an accident.

- Pay out the remaining balance: There will be some savings to the estate if the balance is paid off. As with the above, the estate keeps the car and returns it at the end of the lease. There is the same liability issue with this option as continuing the lease payments.

- Return the car: You can return the car to the lessor. They will sell it at auction and the estate will be liable for the remaining balance.

- Transfer the lease: Check with the leasing company to see if this is possible.

- Insurance Payoff of Lease: Check to see if there is a Credit Life Disability Insurance policy that covers the lease payments for the car. This is a policy specifically designed to pay off the lease in the event of the person's death. It is in essence a term life insurance policy for the term of the lease and in the amount of the lease in decreasing amounts.

The one overarching goal when disposing of the car is to *limit the liability of the estate* to any risk an accident may cause.

Chapter 19

Closing the Estate

Bank accounts have been closed, the house has been sold, and distribution of the possessions has been agreed to. Now it comes time to close the estate.

It is a simple, straightforward, and somewhat anticlimactic event to close the estate. As executor, you will let your attorney know that there is no other work to do. The attorney will ensure the following:

- All estate accounts are closed.
- A final accounting is prepared and filed with the court.
- Beneficiaries have signed a refunding bond and release.
- The refunding bond and release is filed with the surrogate court.

The final accounting is a record of all money paid out and taken in by the estate, including disbursement to the beneficiaries. See page 50 for more information on the final accounting.

The beneficiaries will sign the refunding bond. This legally binds them to give back an equal share of their inheritance should any just debts arise after the inheritance is paid out.

The refunding bonds will be filed with the surrogate court.

The final consideration before the estate can be closed is taxes. Estate tax returns and possibly personal income tax returns will need to be filed and any tax paid before the estate can be finally closed out. This may take anywhere from one month to one year, depending on tax laws in force at the time and the state in which they are filed. Estate tax will need to be paid on any monies the estate realized as income. These monies could be in the form of stock dividends, simple bank interest, or stock gains (or losses). The best course of action is to hire a certified public accountant to prepare these returns for you.

Once tax returns are filed, accepted, and paid and the signed refunding bonds are filed with the court, the estate is closed. You are relieved from your duties as the executor.

It's really not all that difficult to close out an estate. If you don't get too emotionally attached, and treat it as business, you should be able to get past some of the infighting between and among beneficiaries. Above all, you should act fairly, morally, and ethically in everything you do. Just use the "what would a reasonable person do" test when faced with a particular perplexing situation. When seeking advice, you will want to talk to CPAs, lawyers, friends, and even your local clergy to make sure you are doing the right thing. At the end of the day, it's not all about the money, and it's not about who gets what things. It's about making sure the wishes of the person who died are carried out according to their instructions. Good luck!

Chapter 20

What Should I Do If?

We're always getting the question, "What should I do if "*this*" happens?" We hope the following will answer some of those questions and guide you during situations that don't always come up routinely.

What should I do . . .

. . . if one of the beneficiaries doesn't sign the refunding bond?

The most likely reason is that the beneficiary doesn't think the distribution is fair. Your first attempt should be to discuss the reason, try to compromise, and see if a solution can be worked out. If the difference is irreconcilable, withhold that person's portion of the estate distribution until the bond is signed. This will keep the estate open; however, it may be worth the leverage of withholding monies to incent them to sign off on the bond. If it's as simple as needing an explanation of what a refunding bond is, you might want to have that person talk to the estate lawyer to help them understand.

. . . if someone sues the estate?

Gather up as many facts as you can, determine if the suit is legitimate, and engage the services of an attorney if you don't have one already. This may be costly but in the long run worthwhile. Most likely the suit will come from someone who believes the person who passed away owed them money and there is some discrepancy.

. . . if someone says they should be the executor instead of me?

If you're named in the filed will, you are the executor. If that other person still believes that they are the legitimate executor of the will, they can petition the surrogate court for a change. This almost never happens.

. . . if the house was already under a sales contract and my loved one passed away before the sale was complete?

In almost every case, you will continue with the sale. All you'll need to do is probate the will and obtain the necessary letters testamentary, and the sale will go through as if your loved one was still alive. In unique cases, the sale can be voided and you can find a new buyer if you so choose. It works the same way for a car and other big-ticket items.

. . . if I really don't want to be the executor?

Most states simply have you fill out a form that you send to the surrogate/probate court that allows you to renounce your role as executor. You sign, notarize, and return it, and you are no longer responsible for administration of the estate. Some states require that you personally renounce your role by signing in front of them at their office. Check with the surrogate court in your state/county.

. . . if someone accuses me of hiding assets or misappropriating funds?

Don't worry all too much about that. You can and should (assuming they are a beneficiary) show them an accounting of the finances you've done up to that date. If they still have an issue, they can file with the surrogate court and the court will ask you to provide the accounting. Make sure you comply with the request within the allotted time frame. Most likely you will have nothing to worry about as long as you accurately accounted for all the assets and liabilities of the estate.

. . . if someone who isn't a beneficiary asks me what was in the will?

You don't need to tell them anything; politely tell them that you're not able to provide that information.

. . . if someone says they'll get a copy of the will from the surrogate or probate court?

That is their right. A will is a public record once it is filed, and as such, anyone has the right to obtain a copy. So, if someone wants to see what your aunt Sally left her next-door neighbor (assuming it's in the will), they can write to the court and see what's in there.

. . . if a spouse or child was not in the will?

A child and/or spouse may be able to challenge the will if the decedent excluded them. You would need to confer with a lawyer to understand your options.

. . . if the will was written by a lawyer in one state but is being filed in another state?

This could happen if your loved one lived, let's say, in New Jersey and had their will written by a New Jersey lawyer and then moved to Florida years later and didn't change the will. Generally, as long as the will was written in accordance with the laws of the state of New Jersey at the time, the will is valid and can be probated in Florida. This relates to the "full faith and credit" clause of the U.S. Constitution.

Final Thoughts

One final chapter dedicated to mistakes that executors make and some of the things that they forget follow:

Some of the more significant items that executors forget:

- There are a few come to mind. As discussed in previous chapters, vacant real estate carries a greater risk with insurance firms and the firm may not cover loss if the home has been vacant for more than 'x' (typically 30) days. That's important because It carries the greatest risk of loss to the estate in most cases.

- It's very important in understanding that income tax must be filed for the tax year the person was living and then the estate must also file taxes. It's a concept that most don't grasp right off the bat. In essence it's two tax returns, one for the person and one for the estate.

- It's a small one but one always forgotten – canceling the Cable TV service. In some instances, it's over $300 per month in cost and the meter will continue to run regardless if anyone is watching - every little bit helps.

- Informing the Social Security Administration that their loved one passed and that there is a death benefit for a spouse. The funeral home usually reports to the SSA but it's important to remember.

- Not keeping accurate records. The benefit is two-fold; reimbursement for the executor for out-of-pocket expenses that come up - including mileage and savings for the estate on taxes, i.e. probate cost, attorney fees, CPA fee's, etc....

- And the last main mistake that is made is the executor thinking that they'll be wrapped up in a month. The most likely scenario is that it will take more than a year even to close a simple estate.

- Make sure all deadlines are met, especially those relating to federal, state and local forms - and fill them out completely. Ask for help if you need it, you might be pleasantly surprised at how helpful the government is now vs. "the old days".

One other item for consideration is that when a will is written by the last living parent and that parent has multiple children, more often than not the executor duties are split between or among those children. The rational is not excluding one child over another - no favoritism. There has been a situation that we are aware of where co-executors are in place because of a trust issue - it's always not wanting to exclude. Bad idea. It slows the process down because each of the co-executors can't act independently, they have to act together. This slows down every interaction where a signature is required because paperwork has to travel back and forth. So if the children who are all beneficiaries are all reasonable people and can act fairly - there should only be one executor. As a personal example, my wife is one of 2 siblings, she has a sister in Florida. Her mother has co-executrix's and chose that because of the "I can't exclude" rational. My wife and her sister both don't care if it's one or the other – both are rational and both realize that it's more work if they are co-executrix's but their mother can't bring herself to make that change. They'll either have to sign jointly and overnite/mail paperwork or one will need to relinquish the right to administer the estate. It would just be easier if it's one or the other from a purely administrative standpoint

The one question that you may want to know the answer to is: "How do I know if I did a good job". And that's a very difficult question to answer as there is no empirical measurement that you can gauge against. The best answer that we've found is that if the beneficiaries are still talking after the estate is closed and nothing during the closing came between them – that is the best measure of success an executor can hope for.

One final note. If you have any feedback either positive or suggestions for improvement or would like to share your executor story for inclusion in the next edition - please feel free to send an e-mail to kjgrube@executorbook.com or go to our website https://www.executorbook.com. Thank you and Good Luck!

APPENDICES

Appendix A – Checklist for Funeral Arrangements

Item	Description/Narrative
Funeral Home	Select the funeral home,
Viewings	One day, two viewings, two viewing days, etc. . . . time of the viewing
Funeral Card	Decedent's name; date of birth/death; short verse, passage, or poem descriptive of the person's life
Music at Funeral	What would your loved one have liked?
Church or Synagogue	Which church or synagogue is preferred?
Priest, Minister, Rabbi	Is there a trusted or favored member of the clergy?
Special Songs	Songs the deceased would have liked
Type of Casket	Varies widely, both type and cost
Limo Service	For family
Flower Car	Perhaps it's not needed.
Special Requests	For example, bagpipes, suits for pallbearers, etc.
Casket Interior	Whatever is suitable and matches the exterior and clothing
Pallbearers	You'll need to pay for pallbearers from the funeral home if you don't designate family or friends.
Burial Clothing	In today's funeral settings, whatever you feel the deceased would be comfortable with
Pictures at viewing	Ask everyone to share a favorite picture and display them all prominently; don't leave anyone out.
Obituary	Read some recent obituaries and follow the format you feel is most appropriate.
Thank-you Cards	Must be sent for monetary gifts, flowers, and Mass cards. Discretionary for sympathy cards. You may want to print them with your loved one's name.
"In Lieu of" Requests	For example, "In lieu of flowers, please send donations to ABC Foundation."
Cremation or Interment	Or burial at sea or ashes scattered or interment in a national cemetery if applicable.
Memorial Service Only	
Exclusions	If your loved one wanted anyone to be specifically

Item	Description/Narrative
	excluded at the viewing or service, make that known to the funeral director. They are not bouncers however and they will be able to help guide you through how to handle one you would prefer excluded. Otherwise all should be welcome to pay their final respects.
Headstone	Consider the type, size, epitaph, stone, etc.
Luncheon/Repast	If you would like a repast after the funeral, where, etc.

Appendix B: Legal References

American Bar Association:	www.abanet.org
Martindale Hubble:	www.martindale.com
Securities Transfer Association	www.stai.org
State of New Jersey:	www.state.nj.us
State governments:	www.state.xx.us[16]
Securities and Exchange Commission (SEC)	www.sec.gov

[16]Where "xx" represents the state abbreviation

Appendix C: Other Resources

Loans against the estate:	The Suburban Group
Jewelry	www.midwestgems.com
Selling a Car	www.carcash.com www.carbuyersusa.com www.carvana.com
Donating a Car	www.cancer.org
Salvation Army	www.salvationarmyusa.org
U.S. Veterans Administration	www.va.gov

Appendix D: Transfer Agents

Members of the Society of Transfer Agents. Source: Securities Transfer Association

- Action Stock Transfer Corp.
- Aflac Incorporated
- AllianceBernstein L.P.
- Amboy National Bank
- Ameren Services Company
- American Stock Transfer & Trust Company
- Amundi Pioneer
- AST Trust Company of Canada
- BancFirst
- Banco Popular
- Bank of New York Mellon
- Bank of the Ozarks
- BlockAgent Inc.
- BNY Mellon Investment Servicing (US)
- Boston Financial Data Services, Inc.
- Broadridge Corp Issuer Solutions, Inc.
- Citibank, N.A.
- ClearTrust, LLC
- Colonial Stock Transfer
- Columbia Threadneedle Investments
- Community Trust Bank, Inc.
- Computershare
- Continental Stock Transfer & Trust Co.
- DB Services Americas, Inc.
- Delaware Trust Company
- DST Systems, Inc.
- DTE Energy Company
- Dupree & Company Inc.
- DWS Service Company
- Eastern Caribbean Central Securities Registry
- Eaton Vance Management
- Empire Stock Transfer Inc.
- Entoro Capital
- EQ by Equiniti
- Equity Stock Transfer LLC
- Fidelity Investments
- First Guaranty Bank
- First-Knox National Bank
- FIS Investor Services LLC
- Franklin Templeton Investor Services, LLC
- Globex Transfer, LLC
- Harbor Services Group, Inc.
- Hickory Point Bank & Trust, fsb.
- HSBC Bank USA, N. A.
- IBM Corporation
- Invesco Investment Services, Inc.
- Isabella Bank Corporation
- Island Stock Transfer
- John Hancock Signature Services
- JP Morgan Chase
- Kansas City Life
- MGE Energy, Inc.
- Mountain Share Transfer LLC
- MUFG Union Bank, N.A.
- National Financial Services LLC
- Nevada Agency and Transfer Company
- New Horizon Transfer, Inc.
- Northern Trust Company
- Odyssey Trust
- Old Second National Bank of Aurora
- Olde Monmouth Stock Transfer Co., Inc.
- Olympia Trust Company
- Otter Tail Corporation
- Pacific Stock Transfer Company
- Philadelphia Stock Transfer, Inc.
- Phoenix Transfer, Inc.
- Publix Super Markets, Inc.
- RBC Capital Markets, LLC
- Regions Bank
- Rydex Fund Services
- Securities Transfer Corporation
- Securrency
- Sedona Equity Registrar & Transfer
- Shenandoah Telecommunications
- Signature Stock Transfer,

Appendix D: Transfer Agents		
Members of the Society of Transfer Agents. Source: Securities Transfer Association		
Duke Energy	Insurance Co. Manhattan Transfer Registrar Co. Meeder Investment Management, Inc. MFS Service Center, Inc.	Inc. Silicon Prairie Registrar & Transfer SmartStop Asset Management
WSFS Bank Zions First National Bank		Southern Stock Transfer Company, LLC Standard Registrar & Transfer Co., Inc. Starion Bond Services State Street Bank and Trust Company State Treasurer Office - Kansas T. Rowe Price TMI Trust Company Transamerica Fund Services, Inc. Transfer Online, Inc. TSX Trust Company U. S. Bancorp Fund Services, LLC U.S. Bank N.A. Ultimus Fund Solutions, LLC UMB Fund Services, Inc. UTG, Inc. Vertalo VStock Transfer LLC Walt Disney Company Wells Fargo Bank, N.A. West Coast Stock Transfer Inc. Wilmington Trust Company Worldwide Stock Transfer, LLC

Appendix D: Transfer Agents		
Members of the Society of Transfer Agents. Source: Securities Transfer Association		

Appendix E: Sample Homeowners Insurance Refund Letter

Your Name

Street
City, State Zip

Date

Person's Name
Insurance Company Name
Street
City, State Zip

Reference: Estate of "deceased"
Policy Number: "policy number"

Dear Ms. or Mr. xxxxx,

The home the above policy represents (***street, city, state, zip of decedent's home***) was sold on ***date***. Would you kindly cancel the policy as of that date.

At your earliest convenience please initiate a prorated refund, making the check payable to "Estate of ***name of deceased,***" and mail to me at the above address.

Please do not hesitate to contact me at ***phone number*** should you have any questions.

Sincerely,

your name, Executor

Appendix F: Sample Automobile Insurance Refund Letter

your name
street
city, state, zip

date

agent's name (if known)
insurance company name
street
city, state, zip

Reference: Estate of ***(decedent's name)***, Policy Number: ***(number)***

Dear ***(agent's name)*** or Sir or Madam,

Please cancel the auto insurance for the car referenced by the above policy effective immediately. The car was sold on ***(date)***.

Attached is a photocopy of the letters testamentary. Please send a prorated refund made payable to "Estate of ***(decedent's name)***" at your earliest convenience to the address above.

Please do not hesitate to contact me at ***(your phone #)*** should you have any questions.

Sincerely,

(your name)–Executor

Appendix G: Sample Letter of Instruction for Securities

Your Name
street
City, State, Zip

date
Transfer Agent Name
street
City, State, Zip

Reference: **Letter of Instruction**, Stock Transfer, Estate of ***decedent's name–Social Security Number*** for ***security name***

Dear Sir or Madam,

Enclosed are the forms you require for the transfer of stock from a deceased individual stockholder. Also enclosed is certificate #**xxxxx** representing **xx** shares of common stock (if applicable).

Please transfer shares as indicated. There are **x** beneficiaries for the above referenced estate; all are children of the deceased. The shares are to be divided equally among the beneficiaries, including fractional shares, as follows:

Beneficiary Name	**SSN**	**Transfer Securities To**	**Account #**	**DTC #**
name	**SS #**	**Name of Institution**	**xxx-xxxx**	**xxxx**

If you have any questions, please do not hesitate to contact me at ***phone number*/e-mail** during business hours.

Sincerely,

your name, Executor

Appendix H: Sample Stock Power Form

Stock/Bond Power

For value received, the undersigned does (do) hereby sell, assign. and transfer to:

Beneficiary name(s) **Social Security #** **Street, City, State, Zip (see note 1)**

(see note 2) certificate shares or bonds represented by certificate numbers ***(see note 3)*** and/or ***(see note 4)*** bank-held shares held for you in account number ***(see note 5)*** of the ***(see note 6)*** stock/bond of ***(see note 7)*** standing in the name(s) of the undersigned on the books of said Company, and hereby irrevocably constitute and appoint ***(see note 8)*** , attorney, to transfer said stock or bond(s) as the case may be on the books of said Company, with full power of substitution in the premises.

If this transfer does not change the beneficial owner(s) or Social Security/taxpayer identification number, the dividend reinvestment plan will continue. If the transfer results in a change of the beneficial owner(s), an authorization to enroll in the dividend reinvestment plan must be submitted by the new owner(s) of the shares unless the new owner(s) is currently a dividend reinvestment plan participant.

Dated _____*(see_note 9)*_______________

IMPORTANT—READ CAREFULLY ***(see note 10)***
Signature must be Medallion Guaranteed by a SIGNATURE OF CURRENT
REGISTERED Financial Institution that is a member of The OWNER OR LEGAL
REPRESENTATIVE
Securities Transfer Association Medallion
Program, or Stock Exchange Medallion Program. ***(see note 11)***
SIGNATURE OF CURRENT REGISTERED LEGAL
REPRESENTATIVE (IF MORE THAN ONE)

MEDALLION GUARANTEE
TO BE AFFIXED HERE

Explanation of Notes

Note 1: Simply the name, Social Security Number, and current address of the beneficiaries. If more than one, continue to list them.

Note 2: The number of shares you have in a physical certificate form. Add up the number of shares listed on the front of the certificate. If there are none, write **(NONE)**.

Note 3: The certificate number(s) on the face of each certificate. If there are none, write **(NONE)**.

Note 4: These are the shares held in book entry form. Write the number of shares to divide; most likely it will be all the shares held and how the split should occur. If all the beneficiaries share equally, write in **"All, divided equally."**

Note 5: Simply the account number from the transfer agent statement.

Note 6: The type of stock, usually common stock, possibly preferred stock. The type of stock will usually be noted on the statement.

Note 7: The name of the company the stock is in.

Note 8: The name of the transfer agent.

Note 9: Date you signed the power; date it in front of Medallion guarantor.

Note 10: Your signature as executor/trix; sign in front of Medallion guarantor.

Note 11: If there is a co-executor or there are co-executors; sign in front of Medallion guarantor.

Appendix I: Sample Stock Power Form

Completed Example

Below is a completed stock power form with two beneficiaries for an estate that has 125 shares of IBM common stock, 25 in certificate form and 100 in book entry form. The account number is 1234-5678, and the transfer agent is First Chicago Securities (Date and signature sections not included.)

Appendix J: Sample Affidavit of Domicile

STATE OF **(state you reside in)**)
) SS:
COUNTY OF **(county you reside in)**)

I, ***(your name)***, being duly sworn, deposed and say that I reside at ***(your current address)*** and acting as the ***Executor or Executrix*** of the Estate of ***(name of deceased)***, Deceased, who died in the State of ***(state person died in)*** on the ***(day of death)*** day in the month of ***(month, year)***; that at the time of ***his or her*** death the domicile (legal residence) was at ***(address where the person lived when he/she died)***.

That all debts of and taxes and claims against the decedent's Estate have been paid or provided for; that this affidavit is made for purposes of securing the transfer or delivery of property owned by the decedent at the time of his/her death to a purchaser or the person or persons legally entitled thereto under the laws of decedent's domicile; and that any apparent inequality in distribution has been satisfied or provided for out of other assets of the Estate.

Sworn to and subscribed before me

This _______ day of _____, ______

____

Signature

____
Notary Public
My Commission Expires ***(YOUR NAME)***
Executor

Appendix K: Sample Refunding Bond

This is a sample of the letter your lawyer will prepare for the beneficiaries to sign indicating they will pay the estate back should any just debt arise after monies have been distributed.

SAMPLE REFUNDING BOND AND RELEASE

IN THE MATTER OF THE ESTATE OF:
____ ***(name of deceased)*** ______________________________ :
DECEASED

KNOWN ALL MEN BY THESE PRESENTS, That I
(name of beneficiary) Obligor

residing at: _____ ***(address of beneficiary)*** ______________________

am hereby held and firmly bound unto ***(Name of Executor or Administrator)*** Obligee in the sum of **$ ___(amount beneficiary received from estate)__** lawful money of the United States of America, to be paid to the Obligee or to Obligee's certain Attorney, successors in office or assigns, for which payment well and truly to be made I bind myself, my heirs, executors, and administrators firmly by these presents. Sealed with my seal and dated the **_(day)___** of ***_(month) (year).***

The condition of the above Obligation is such that whereas the Obligor has received from the Obligee: ***$ (monies received)*** And in Consideration Therefore, the Obligor has remised, released, and forever discharged and by these presents does remise, release, and forever discharge the Obligee from all claims and demands whatsoever, in law or in equity, on account of or in respect to the estate of said deceased and of Obligor's interest therein.

Now Therefore, if the Obligor be a devise, then and in that case if any part or the whole of such devise shall at any time hereafter appear to be wanting to discharge and debt(s), devise or devises, which the said executor or administrator may not have other assets to pay, the Obligor will return said devise or such part thereof as may be necessary for the payment of said debts or for the payment of a proportional part of the said devises; or

If the Obligor be a distributee, then and in that case if any debt(s), truly owing by the intestate, shall be afterward sued for and recovered or otherwise duly made to appear, and which there shall be no other assets to pay, Obligor shall refund and pay back to the administrator, the Obligor's ratable part of such debt(s), out of the part and share so allotted to the Obligor.
The above obligation to be void, or else to be and remain in full force and virtue.

The words "debt(s)" wherever used herein shall be deemed to include all taxes imposed upon or chargeable to the estate or owed by the deceased, including but not limited to Federal, New Jersey or other State or Sovereignty transfer inheritance, estate, death, transfer, and income taxes, together with interest, penalties, costs, expenses, and counsel fees, if any.

Sworn to and subscribed before me

This _______ day of _____, ______

____

____

Notary Public
My Commission Expires:

Appendix L: Sample Spreadsheet to Track Stocks

Estate of (Deceased's Name) - Securities Information Stock Value At Close of Trading on month, day, year							
Stock or Bond	**Ticker**	**# of Shares**	**25% of Total Shares**	**Price Per Share***	**Total Value**	**Held by**	**Other Information**
AT&T	T	282.0000	70.5000	$ 20.87	$ 5,885.34	Schwab	
AT&T Wireless	AWE	90.0000	22.5000	$ 16.95	$ 1,525.50	Schwab	Spinoff on 7/9/02
Avaya	AV	10.0000	2.5000	$ 13.70	$ 137.00	Schwab	
Disney	DIS	1,000.0000	250.0000	$ 28.19	$ 28,190.00	Schwab	
Lucent	LU	120.0000	30.0000	$ 7.33	$ 879.60	Schwab	
Primesource	PSRC	45.0000	11.2500	$ 4.33	$ 194.85	Schwab	
Qwest	Q	112.0000	28.0000	$ 29.52	$ 3,306.24	Schwab	
SBC Comm	SBC	189.0000	47.2500	$ 41.95	$ 7,928.55	Schwab	
Verizon	VZ	188.0000	47.0000	$ 55.25	$ 10,387.00	Schwab	
Vodafone	VOD	155.0000	38.7500	$ 21.61	$ 3,349.55	Schwab	
Zany Brainy	ZANY	6,165.0000	1,541.2500	$ -	$ -	Schwab	Chapter 11
Verizon	VZ	73.5161	18.3790	$ 55.25	$ 4,061.76	Transfer Agent - Equiserv	www.equiserve.com
Bell South	BLS	359.1093	89.7773	$ 40.03	$ 14,375.15	98 Certificate, 261. TA Mellon	www.chasemellon.com
NCR	NCR	11.7500	2.9375	$ 40.28	$ 473.29	Transfer Agent - AMStock	www.investpower.com
SBC Comm**	SBC	234.0000	58.5000	$ 41.95	$ 9,816.30	Transfer Agent - Equiserv	www.equiserve.com
Lucent	LU	120.0000	30.0000	$ 7.33	$ 879.60	Transfer Agent - BoNY	www.stockbny.com
Avaya	AV	10.0000	2.5000	$ 13.70	$ 137.00	Transfer Agent - BoNY	www.stockbny.com
					$ 91,526.73		
*Source:	Yahoo Finance (www.yahoo.com) - Stock History by Day						

Appendix M: Sample Asset Tracking Spreadsheet

Summary Asset List - Estate of (Deceased's Name)

SSN: xxx-xx-xxxx

Description	Account Type	Account Number	Est. Value	Last Statement	Contact Name	Contact Number	Notes
Bank Account	Checking	408538219	$1,200.00	6/19/2001	Tom	xxx xxx-xxxx	any notes here
Bank Account	Savings	8500701230	$3,560.39	8/16/2001	Rich	xxx xxx-xxxx	
Bank Account	CD	8500615128	$34,676.40	8/16/2001	Rich	xxx xxx-xxxx	
Brokerage	Mutual Fund	0010 5594 6567	$12,205.00	6/26/2001	Wayne	xxx xxx-xxxx	
Brokerage	Mutual Fund	0011 2594 6567	$11,813.00	6/26/2001	Wayne	xxx xxx-xxxx	
Brokerage	Mutual Fund	0012 2594 6567	$11,436.00	6/26/2001	Wayne	xxx xxx-xxxx	
Brokerage	Mutual Fund	0012 5594 6567	$8,614.00	6/26/2001	Wayne	xxx xxx-xxxx	
Brokerage	Certificate	0080 0952 5506	$9,661.00	6/26/2001	Wayne	xxx xxx-xxxx	
Brokerage	Account Name	3944-3641-234	$65,000.00	6/30/2001	Bill	xxx xxx-xxxx	
Toyota Corolla	Auto	n/a	$11,000.00	n/a	Bill	xxx xxx-xxxx	
Company Name	Stock	xxx-xx-xxxx	$446.50	12/13/1996	Bill	xxx xxx-xxxx	
Company Name	Stock	001 752 079	$14,501.00	7/16/2001	Bill	xxx xxx-xxxx	
Company Name	Stock	9172-6117-863	$4,061.76	2/1/2001	Bill	xxx xxx-xxxx	
Company Name	Stock	754387234	$879.60	2/5/2001	Bill	xxx xxx-xxxx	
Company Name	Stock	754383424	$137.00	9/20/2001	Bill	xxx xxx-xxxx	
Company Name	Stock	7498-30596 AS	$9,816.30	4/10/2001	Bill	xxx xxx-xxxx	
		TOTAL:	$199,007.95				

Last Modified: month, day, year

Appendix N: Sample Expense Tracking Spreadsheet

Miscellaneous Reimbursable Expenses								
Reimburse To	Amount	Purchase Date	Payee	Reason	Receipt?	Date Paid	Check Number	Submitted to Lawyer
Name	$ 20.00	mm/dd/yy	Payee Name	Tip for Art - Oxy Set-Up	no	mm/dd/yy		mm/dd/yy
Name	$ 7.07	mm/dd/yy	Payee Name	For Supplies (notepad and envelopes)	yes	"		"
Name	$ 431.87	mm/dd/yy	Payee Name	Dinner/Brick House	yes	"		"
Name	$ 14.28	mm/dd/yy	Payee Name	Moving Boxes - Office Depot (all bene's)	yes	"		"
Name	$ 53.00	mm/dd/yy	Payee Name	Brick House	yes	"		"
Name	$ 19.05	mm/dd/yy	Payee Name	For Supplies (folder and Moving Boxes)	yes	"		"
Name	$ 14.76	mm/dd/yy	Payee Name	Garbage Bags	yes	"		"
Name	$ 100.63	mm/dd/yy	Payee Name	Paper Products for after funeral lunch	yes	"		"
Name	$ 150.00	mm/dd/yy	Payee Name	Waitress Fee and Tip for funeral lunch	no	"		"
Name	$ 2.97	mm/dd/yy	Payee Name	Copies of will for all and 1 extra	yes	"		"
Name	$ 1.80	mm/dd/yy	Payee Name	Copies of will for Bank	yes	"		"
Name	$ 500.00	mm/dd/yy	Payee Name	Carpenter, Fix Joist Termite Damage	no	"		"
TOTAL:	$ 1,315.43							

You can use this sheet to track any reimbursable expenses for the estate.

Reimburse To:	The name of the person who used their funds for the expenditure
Amount:	The amount of the expense
Purchase date:	Date the item or service was purchased
Payee:	The person or company name who provided the item or service
Reason: needed	A short description of why the expense was
Receipt?	Was a receipt provided? (yes/no) If no and over $75, make a footnote about why the receipt is not available (for tax purposes).
Date Paid:	The date the reimbursement check was received from the lawyer
Check Number	The number of the check paid by the estate
Submitted to Lawyer	Date the reimbursement request was submitted to the lawyer

Appendix O: Mileage and Time Tracking Spreadsheets

Mileage Tracking Sheet - Estate of ___________

Date	From	To	Miles Driven	Purpose
10/12/2011	Washingtonville, NJ	Belleville, NJ	23	File estate paperwork with surrogate
10/12/2011	Belleville, NJ	Washingtonville, NJ	23	Return Trip
10/25/2011	Washintonville, NJ	New York, NY	18	Meet with estate Attorney
10/25/2011	New York, NY	Washintonville, NJ	18	Return Trip

Total Miles Driven:		82
Reimbursement per mile:	$	0.51
Total Reimbursement:		41.82

Appendix P: Sample Notice to Beneficiaries

Your Name
Street
City, State, Zip

Date

Beneficiary Name
Street
City, State, Zip

Reference: Estate of [name of deceased] Notice to Beneficiary

Dear Ms or Mr. xxxxx,

Please be advised that you are a beneficiary named in the Last Will and Testament of **[name of deceased]**. A copy of the will is attached.

Please do not hesitate to contact me at ***[phone number] or e-mail [username@xxx.com}*** should you have any questions.

Sincerely,

[your name]**,**
Executor

GENERAL INFORMATION SHEET

APPLICATION FOR STANDARD GOVERNMENT HEADSTONE OR MARKER FOR INSTALLATION IN A PRIVATE CEMETERY OR A STATE VETERANS' CEMETERY

RESPONDENT BURDEN - Public reporting burden for this collection of information is estimated to average one-fourth hour per response, including the time for reviewing instructions, searching existing data sources, gathering and maintaining the data needed, and completing and reviewing the collection of information. VA may not conduct or sponsor, and the respondent is not required to respond to this information collection unless it displays a valid OMB Control Number. Response is required to obtain benefit. Send comments regarding this burden estimate or any other aspect of this collection of information, including suggestions for reducing this burden to the VA Clearance Officer (005R1B), 810 Vermont Avenue, NW, Washington, DC 20420. Please DO NOT send applications for benefits to this address.

BENEFIT PROVIDED

a. HEADSTONE OR MARKER

For deaths occurring on or after November 1, 1990 - Furnished upon application for the grave of any eligible deceased veteran. Will be provided regardless of whether or not the grave is already marked with a privately purchased headstone or marker. Applicant may be anyone having knowledge of the deceased.

For deaths occurring before November 1, 1990 - Furnished upon application for the **UNMARKED GRAVE** of any eligible deceased veteran. The individual must certify the grave is **unmarked** and a Government headstone or marker is preferred to a privately purchased headstone or marker. **A grave is considered marked if a monument displays the decedent's name and date of birth and/or death, even though the veteran's military data is not shown**. Applicant may be anyone having knowledge of the deceased.

b. MEMORIAL HEADSTONE OR MARKER - Furnished upon application **for installation in a cemetery only** to commemorate any eligible veteran whose remains have not been recovered or identified, were buried at sea, donated to science, or cremated and the remains scattered; may not be used as a memento. Check box in block 28 and explain in block 27. Applicant may be anyone having knowledge of the deceased.

WHO IS ELIGIBLE - Any deceased veteran discharged under conditions other than dishonorable. A copy of the deceased veteran's discharge certificate (DD Form 214 or equivalent) or a copy of other official document(s) establishing military service must be attached. **Do not send original documents**; they will not be returned. **Service after September 7, 1980, must be for a minimum of 24 months continuous active duty or be completed under special circumstances, e.g., death on active duty**. Persons who have only limited active duty service for training while in the National Guard or Reserves are not eligible unless there are special circumstances, e.g., death while on active duty, or as a result of training. Reservists and National Guard members who, at time of death, were entitled to retired pay, or would have been entitled, but for being under the age of 60, are eligible; a copy of the Reserve Retirement Eligibility Benefits Letter must accompany the application. Reservists called to active duty and National Guard members who are Federalized and who serve for the period called are eligible. Service prior to World War I requires detailed documentation, e.g., muster rolls, extracts from State files, military or State organization where served, pension or land warrant, etc.

HOW TO APPLY

FAX applications and supporting documents to **1-800-455-7143**.
IMPORTANT: If faxing more than one application - fax each application package (application plus supporting documents) individually i.e., disconnect the call and redial for each submission.

MAIL applications to: **Memorial Programs Service (41A1)**
Department of Veterans Affairs
5109 Russell Road
Quantico, VA 22134-3903

A Government headstone or marker may be furnished only upon receipt of a fully completed and signed application with required supporting documentation.

SIGNATURES REQUIRED - The person responsible for the information on this form signs in block 17; the person agreeing to accept delivery (consignee) in block 22, and the cemetery or other responsible official in block 24. If there is no official on duty at the cemetery, the signature of the person responsible for the property listed in block 21 is required. Entries of "None," "Not Applicable," or "NA" cannot be accepted. State Veterans' Cemeteries are not required to complete blocks 17, 18, 22 and 23.

ASSISTANCE NEEDED - If assistance is needed to complete this application, contact the nearest VA Regional Office, national cemetery, or a local veterans' organization. No fee should be paid in connection with the preparation of this application. Use block 27 for any clarification or other information you wish to provide. Should you have questions when filling out this form, you may contact our Applicant Assistance Unit toll free at: 1-800-697-6947, or via e-mail at mps.headstones@va.gov *For more information regarding headstones and markers visit our website at www.cem.va.gov.*

INSTALLATION - The Government is not responsible for costs to install the headstone or marker in private cemeteries.

TRANSPORTATION AND DELIVERY OF MARKER - The headstone or marker is shipped without charge to the consignee designated in block 19 of the application. **The delivery will not be made to a Post Office box.** The consignee should be a business with full delivery address and telephone number. If the consignee is not a business explain fully in block 27. For delivery to a Rural Route address, you must include a daytime telephone number including area code in block 20. If you fail to include the required address and telephone number information, we cannot deliver the marker.

CAUTION - To avoid delays in the production and delivery of the headstone or marker, please check carefully to be sure you have accurately furnished all required information before faxing or mailing the application. Mistakes cannot be corrected after a headstone or marker has been ordered. Headstones or markers furnished remain the property of the United States Government and may not be used for any purpose other than to honor the memory of the decedent for whom the headstone or marker is issued.

DETACH AND RETAIN THIS GENERAL INFORMATION SHEET FOR YOUR RECORDS.

VA FORM AUG 2009 **40-1330** SUPERSEDES VA FORM 40-1330, MAY 2008, WHICH WILL NOT BE USED. Adobe LiveCycle Designer

ILLUSTRATIONS OF STANDARD GOVERNMENT HEADSTONES AND MARKERS

UPRIGHT HEADSTONE
WHITE MARBLE OR
LIGHT GRAY GRANITE

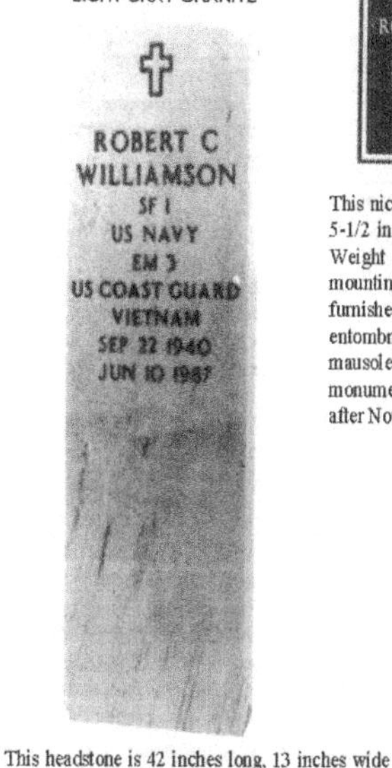

This headstone is 42 inches long, 13 inches wide and 4 inches thick. Weight is approximately 230 pounds. Variations may occur in stone color, and the marble may contain light to moderate veining.

BRONZE NICHE

This niche marker is 8-1/2 inches long, 5-1/2 inches wide, with 7/16 inch rise. Weight is approximately 3 pounds; mounting bolts and washers are furnished with the marker. For use if entombment is in a columbarium or mausoleum, or to supplement a private monument, for deaths occurring on or after November 1, 1990.

FLAT MARKERS

BRONZE

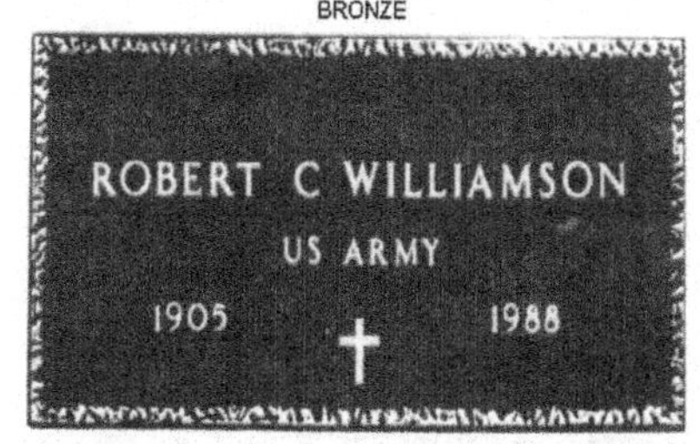

This grave marker is 24 inches long, 12 inches wide, with 3/4 inch rise. Weight is approximately 18 pounds. Anchor bolts, nuts and washers for fastening to a base are furnished with the marker. The base is not furnished by the Government.

LIGHT GRAY GRANITE OR WHITE MARBLE

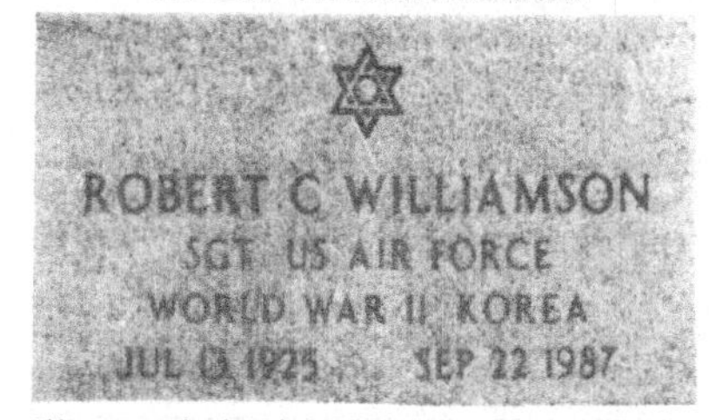

This grave marker is 24 inches long, 12 inches wide, and 4 inches thick. Weight is approximately 130 pounds. Variations may occur in stone color; the marble may contain light to moderate veining.

NOTE: Civil War Era headstones - In addition to the headstone and markers pictured, two special styles of upright headstones are available for those who served with Union Forces during the Civil War or for those who served in the Spanish-American War, and another for those who served with the Confederate States of America during the Civil War. Requests for these special styles should be made in block 27 of the application. It is necessary to submit detailed documentation that supports eligibility.

INSCRIPTION INFORMATION

MANDATORY ITEMS of inscription at Government expense are: Legal Name, Branch of Service, Year of Birth, and Year of Death. Branches of Service are: U.S. Army (USA), U.S. Navy (USN), U.S. Air Force (USAF), U.S. Marine Corps (USMC), U.S. Coast Guard (USCG), and by exception, U.S. Army Air Forces (USAAF), and other parent organizations authorized for certain periods of time and special units such as Women's Army Auxiliary Corps (WAAC), Women's Air Force Service Pilots (WASP), U.S. Public Health Service (USPHS), and National Oceanic & Atmospheric Administration (NOAA). Different examples of inscription formats are illustrated above. More than one branch of service is permitted, subject to space availability.

OPTIONAL ITEMS are identified on the application in boxes with bold outlines. These items may be included at Government expense if desired. Optional items include month and day of birth in block 5A, month and day of death in block 5B, highest rank attained in block 7, awards in block 9, war service in block 10, and emblem of belief in block 12. War service includes active duty service during a recognized period of war and the individual does not have to serve in the actual place of war, i.e. Vietnam may be inscribed if the veteran served during the Vietnam War period, even though the individual never served in Vietnam itself. Supporting documentation must be included with the application if you wish to include the highest rank and/or awards.

RESERVED SPACE for future inscriptions at private expense, such as spousal or dependent data, is allowed if requested in block 27 and if space is available. Only two lines of space may be reserved on flat markers due to space limitations. Reserved space is unnecessary on upright marble or granite headstones as the reverse side is available for future inscriptions.

MEMORIAL HEADSTONES AND MARKERS (remains are not buried). The words "In Memory Of" are mandatory and precede the authorized inscription data. The words "In Memory Of" are not inscribed when remains are buried.

ADDITIONAL ITEMS may be inscribed at government expense if they are requested on the initial application and space is available. Examples of acceptable items include terms of endearment, nicknames (in expressions such as "OUR BELOVED POPPY"), military or civilian credentials or accomplishments such as DOCTOR, REVEREND, etc., and special unit designations such as WOMEN'S ARMY CORPS, ARMY AIR CORPS, ARMY NURSE CORPS or SEABEES. All requests for additional inscription items should be stated in block 27, and are subject to VA approval. No graphics, emblems or pictures are permitted except VA approved emblems of belief, the Medal of Honor, and the Southern Cross of Honor for Civil War Confederate Veterans.

INCOMPLETE OR INACCURATE INFORMATION ON THE APPLICATION MAY RESULT IN ITS RETURN TO THE APPLICANT, A DELAY IN RECEIPT OF THE HEADSTONE OR MARKER, OR AN INCORRECT INSCRIPTION.

Form approved, OMB No. 2900-0222
Respondent Burden: 15 minutes

Department of Veterans Affairs

IMPORTANT: Please read the General Information Sheet before completing this form. Type or print clearly all information except for signatures. Illegible printing could result in an incorrect headstone or marker or delivery. *Blocks outlined in bold are optional inscription items. Unless indicated otherwise* all other blocks **must** be completed. **MILITARY DISCHARGE DOCUMENTS OR RELATED SERVICE INFORMATION IS REQUIRED.**

1. TYPE OF REQUEST
- ☐ INITIAL *(First time)* REQUEST
- ☐ SECOND REQUEST
- ☐ CORRECTED APPLICATION OR REPLACEMENT

2. NAME OF DECEASED TO BE INSCRIBED ON HEADSTONE OR MARKER *(NO NICKNAMES OR TITLES PERMITTED)*

FIRST *(Or Initial)*	MIDDLE *(Or Initial)*	LAST	SUFFIX

3. GRAVE IS:
- ☐ CURRENTLY MARKED *(with privately purchased marker)*
- ☐ NOT MARKED

VETERAN'S SERVICE AND IDENTIFYING INFORMATION *(Use numbers only, e.g., 05-15-1941)*

4. VETERAN'S SOCIAL SECURITY NO. OR SERVICE NO. *(Failure to complete will delay processing.)*

SSN: OR SVC. NO.:

PERIODS OF ACTIVE MILITARY DUTY *(For additional space use Block 27)*

6A. DATE(S) ENTERED			6B. DATE(S) SEPARATED		
MONTH	DAY	YEAR	MONTH	DAY	YEAR

5A. DATE OF BIRTH			5B. DATE OF DEATH		
MONTH	DAY	YEAR	MONTH	DAY	YEAR

7. HIGHEST RANK ATTAINED (No pay grades)

8. BRANCH OF SERVICE *(Check applicable box(es) - must be consistent with rank in Box 7)*

☐ ARMY ☐ NAVY ☐ MARINE CORPS ☐ COAST GUARD ☐ AIR FORCE ☐ ARMY AIR FORCES ☐ MERCHANT MARINE ☐ OTHER *(Specify)*

9. VALOR OR PURPLE HEART AWARD(S) ***(Documentation must be provided)***

☐ MEDAL OF HONOR ☐ DST SVC CROSS ☐ NAVY CROSS ☐ AIR FORCE CROSS ☐ SILVER STAR ☐ BRONZE STAR MEDAL ☐ PURPLE HEART ☐ OTHER *(Specify)*

10. WAR SERVICE *(Check applicable box(es))*

☐ WORLD WAR II ☐ KOREA ☐ VIETNAM ☐ PERSIAN GULF ☐ OTHER *(Specify)*

11. TYPE OF HEADSTONE OR MARKER REQUESTED *(Check one)*

☐ FLAT BRONZE B ☐ FLAT GRANITE G ☐ UPRIGHT MARBLE U ☐ FLAT MARBLE F ☐ BRONZE NICHE Z ☐ UPRIGHT GRANITE V

12. DESIRED EMBLEM OF BELIEF

☐ NONE ☐ EMBLEM NUMBER *(Specify)(See reverse side of this form for authorized emblems)* ______

13A. NAME AND MAILING ADDRESS *(No., Street, City, State, and ZIP Code)* OF PERSON TO CONTACT FOR ADDITIONAL INFORMATION

13B. DAYTIME PHONE NO. OF PERSON TO CONTACT FOR ADDITIONAL INFORMATION

14. E-MAIL ADDRESS *(Optional)*

15. FAX NO. *(Optional)*

16. ARE YOU:
- ☐ NEXT OF KIN
- ☐ CEMETERY OFFICIAL
- ☐ FUNERAL DIRECTOR
- ☐ OTHER *(Specify)*

CERTIFICATION: By signing below I certify the headstone or marker will be installed in the cemetery listed in block 21 at no expense to the Government and all information entered on this form is true and correct to the best of my knowledge.

17. SIGNATURE OF PERSON WHOSE NAME APPEARS IN BLOCK 13A

18. DATE *(MM/DD/YYYY)*

19. NAME AND DELIVERY ADDRESS OF BUSINESS (CONSIGNEE) THAT WILL ACCEPT PREPAID DELIVERY *(No., Street, City, State and ZIP Code)*; ***P.O. BOX IS NOT ACCEPTABLE***

20. DAYTIME PHONE NO. *(Include Area Code)*

21. NAME AND ADDRESS OF CEMETERY WHERE GRAVE IS LOCATED *(No., Street, City, State and ZIP Code)*

CERTIFICATION: By signing below I agree to accept prepaid delivery of the headstone or marker.

22. PRINTED NAME AND SIGNATURE OF PERSON REPRESENTING BUSINESS (CONSIGNEE) NAMED IN BLOCK 19

23. DATE *(MM/DD/YYYY)*

CERTIFICATION: By signing below I certify the type of headstone or marker checked in block 11 is permitted in the cemetery named in block 21.

24. PRINTED NAME AND SIGNATURE OF CEMETERY OR OTHER RESPONSIBLE OFFICIAL

25. DAYTIME PHONE NO. *(Include Area Code)*

26. DATE *(MM/DD/YYYY)*

27. REMARKS *(Optional inscription space will vary in size according to the type of marker)*

28. CHECK BOX BELOW IF REMAINS ARE NOT BURIED AND EXPLAIN IN BLOCK 27 *(e.g., lost at sea, remains scattered, etc.)*
- ☐ REMAINS NOT BURIED

STATE VETERANS' CEMETERY AND GRAVE LOCATION *(Cemetery Use Only)*

29. ID CODE	30. SECTION	31. GRAVE NO.

VA FORM AUG 2009 **40-1330** **APPLICATION FOR STANDARD GOVERNMENT HEADSTONE OR MARKER**

AUTHORIZED EMBLEMS *(See block 12)*

The graphics shown below are of the 20 most requested emblems of belief for placement on government-furnished headstones/markers. The listing below shows all emblems that may be requested.

EMBLEMS OF BELIEF AVAILABLE:

CHRISTIAN CROSS (01)
BUDDHIST (Wheel of Righteousness) (02)
JUDAISM (Star of David) (03)
PRESBYTERIAN CROSS (04)
RUSSIAN ORTHODOX CROSS (05)
LUTHERAN CROSS (06)
EPISCOPAL CROSS (07)
UNITARIAN CHURCH (Flaming Chalice) (08)
UNITED METHODIST CHURCH (09)
AARONIC ORDER CHURCH (10)
MORMON (Angel Moroni) (11)
NATIVE AMERICAN CHURCH OF NORTH AMERICA (12)
SERBIAN ORTHODOX (13)
GREEK CROSS (14)
BAHAI (9 Pointed Star) (15)
ATHEIST (16)
MUSLIM (Crescent and Star) (17)
HINDU (18)
KONKO-KYO FAITH (19)
COMMUNITY OF CHRIST (20)
SUFISM REORIENTED (21)
TENRIKYO CHURCH (22)
SIECHO-NO-IE (23)
THE CHURCH OF WORLD MESSIANITY (Izunome) (24)
UNITED CHURCH OF RELIGIOUS SCIENCE (25)
CHRISTIAN REFORMED CHURCH (26)
UNITED MORAVIAN CHURCH (27)
ECKANKAR (28)
CHRISTIAN CHURCH (29)
CHRISTIAN & MISSIONARY ALLIANCE (30)
UNITED CHURCH OF CHRIST (31)
HUMANIST (American Humanist Association) (32)
PRESBYTERIAN CHURCH (USA) (33)
IZUMO TAISHAKYO MISSION OF HAWAII (34)
SOKA GAKKAI INTERNATIONAL - USA (35)
SIKH (KHANDA) (36)
WICCA (Pentacle) (37)
CHRISTIAN SCIENCE (Cross & Crown) (97)
MUSLIM (Islamic 5 Pointed Star) (98)

This application form is normally updated every two years. To obtain the most recent information about headstones and markers including the complete and most current list of available emblems of belief (listing all names and graphics), please visit our website at www.cem.va.gov. You may also request a copy of this list by contacting our Applicant Assistance unit toll free at 1-800-697-6947, or via e-mail at: mps.headstones@va.gov .

VA FORM 40-1330, AUG 2009

Appendix R Form SS-4, Filing for an Estate Tax ID

Apply online at:

https://irs.usa-taxid.com/products/EINEstate

Index

About the Authors

Kurt Grube takes a practical approach to the challenges he faces and wrote this book because he thought he could help people who were named as executors for the first time. He has been quoted extensively in the May, 2007 AARP article *"How to Be a Good Executor of a Will or Estate"*. [17] Kurt has been quoted in the op-ed pages of *The Record* (Bergen, New Jersey) about pork-barrel spending by Congress and the MF Global bankruptcy. He has appeared on the Fox News Network's *The O'Reilly Factor,* where he gave his no-nonsense opinion about President Clinton and the Monica Lewinsky matter. He is a graduate of Don Bosco High School and William Paterson University (summa cum laude). He is an executive at a large international information technology company and has been certified as a Project Management Professional®[18]. He married his wife Kathy in 1984 and they have 2 grown children.

Keith Grube is an attorney specializing in criminal defense. He has also practiced law in health care operations, fraud and abuse, and done business counseling for an international health care firm. He was a member of the Villanova Law Review, 1990–1992; law clerk to Hon. H. Jonathan Fox, J.S.C., New Jersey, 1992–1993; and co-author with Ivan J. Punchatz of "The Nursing Facility Survey, Certification and Enforcement Regulations," *New Jersey Lawyer, The Magazine,* December 1995; "Learning From Pennsylvania's Experience with 'Dear Provider Letters'—72 Hour DRG Window False Claims Enforcement Project," *New Jersey Law Journal, Health Care Law*

---

[17] https://www.aarp.org/retirement/planning-for-retirement/info-2021/how-to-be-a-good-executor.html - accessed May 10, 2021 author: Sharon Waters

[18] Project Management Institute, www.pmi.org

Supplement, December 18, 1995; and "State Regulators Get Serious About Enforcing Licensure Requirements," *New Jersey Law Journal,* January 22, 1996. He is also the author of "Independent Contractor or Employee? The Rules and Ramifications of Worker Classification in the Health Care Industry," F. Gordon Keckeissen and Keith S. Grube, *Health Law Hand Book,* 1998 ed., West Group, Clark Boardman Callaghan, 1998.

John E. Nevola made his literary debut with *The Last Jump,* a historical novel based on United States airborne operations in Europe during World War II. A retired information technology executive, Nevola has been widely published in business magazines, with numerous articles on disaster recovery and terrorism. In 2011, he commemorated the seventieth anniversary of the sneak attack on Pearl Harbor with *The Revenge of the Pearl Harbor Survivors,* describing the pivotal role played by the American aircraft carriers that survived that despicable attack. In 2018 John published his second novel, *"The Final Flag: Folds of Honor"* which currently has a 5 star rating on Amazon.

Nevola was born in New York City and is a graduate of Cardinal Hayes High School and the College of Aeronautics. He sadly passed away in 2020 after a brief illness.

Acknowledgments

This book could not have been completed without the tireless review of John Nevola and his creative comments. His suggestions and editorial notations (all in red ink, of course) were most gratefully appreciated. The Hon. Jonathan A. Fox was a great inspiration, as was Michael P. Dressler, surrogate judge of Bergen County, New Jersey; Bill O'Reilly from Fox; and Monica Crowley, foreign affairs adviser to President Nixon in the 1990s. Bob and Linda Monaco, Steve Hardek, Crysta Nevola, Chief Robert Herndon (Allendale NJ, Police Department - Ret.) and Susan Herndon all contributed editorial comments, suggestions and encouragement throughout the process.

Many thanks to Laurel Robinson (Laurel Robinson Editorial Services - www.laurelcopyeditor.com) our copyeditor whose insightful recommendations and many, many editorial improvements were much appreciated and much needed.

Last but not at all least is an acknowledgment to Kathy, Kelly, and Chris Grube, whose support and inspiration made the publication of this book a reality.

Back Cover Copy

Have you ever conquered something that you thought would be intimidating but really wasn't all that bad? Being an executor of an estate is one of those things. It's not all that hard to do once you know some of the terminology, forms to use, and filing deadlines. You can easily and quickly accomplish most of the work yourself with a little bit of help and save yourself thousands of dollars in the process. Once you're finished, it's extraordinarily satisfying to know that you carried out your loved one's final wishes.

In this book, Kurt and Keith Grube guide you through the process from the point your loved one passes away, from making funeral arrangements to preparing the final distribution from the estate. They also have recommendations for how to go about the process from a practical standpoint—for example, how to work with your friends and family, fairly dividing the nonmonetary items from the estate, and how to stay organized.

What people are saying:

"Informative and thought-provoking. A must-read for anyone with parents or in-laws in their 70s and 80s. It is a well-organized and easy-to-follow, step-by-step guide." James DeKoek

"This helped me immensely when I was the executrix for my brother's' estate. Because I read the book, I knew what to expect when I worked with my lawyer. I understood the terms he used and how the overall process worked. So that's why the book was valuable to me: I was able to help my lawyer with the estate instead of just letting him tell me 'where to sign.'" Rosalie Barcellona

"Having stumbled through the fact finding, second guessing and self doubt in settling my own Mom's estate...This book is a must read for anyone with aging parents. It is, indeed, a single source of factual information laced with a touch of family interaction techniques that will save countless hours of anxiety while providing the steps to settle all accounts." Bob Monaco

"This guide is very informative and easy to follow. I wish I had a copy available two years ago when my mom passed away. It would have saved me time, money and reduced my frustration level dramatically. I will definitely make sure my sons have a copy for their future reference." Marty Leibowitz

"This book is a must read for anyone who has just lost a loved one. The authors will guide you step by step from the funeral through the complete settling of the estate. They offer advice on how to deal with aggressive lawyers who will attempt to charge egregious rates for mundane tasks that you can execute yourself with the help of this book. They will help you organize your thoughts and walk you through all the steps required to settle the estate including the distribution of all property, jewelry, and other personal belongings. This book can not only help you through the process, but can help

you save considerable money along the way. They also provide example spreadsheets and letters that can easily be customized for your personal use. While losing a love one is a stressful time in one's life, this book can help you navigate through the complicated processes and get you through this difficult time in an efficient, cost-effective manner." Rick Ancona

Made in the USA
Coppell, TX
31 July 2021